TRAGEDY

Of

DECEPTION

(The Taleban as I saw them in *Afghanistan*)

A first hand account of a private sector effort to help alleviate poverty in Afghanistan and the real situation on ground before and after US attack in October 2001

By
Humayun Niaz

Strand Non Fiction

Published 2011 by Strand Publishing UK Ltd.

Golden Cross House, 8 Duncannon Street, Strand

London WC2N 4JF

E-mail address: info@strandpublishing.co.uk

Internet address: www.strandpublishing.co.uk

Paperback ISBN 978-1-907340-13-0

*This book is dedicated
to the people of Afghanistan*

Table of Contents

PREFACE

This is a true and first hand account of the last days of Taliban rule in Afghanistan as seen through the eyes of a neutral, ordinary and non political person who went to Kandahar to set up a flour and general mills in September of the year 2000. All that is said in this book is the absolute truth, and nothing has been concealed. I should also make it clear at the outset that there is no other motive or agenda in writing this, except that the truth must be told. I realize that in today's world controlled by the so-called mainstream media it is not easy. Half-truths and outright lies are being propagated with such force that truth is now a victim of 'collateral damage'. There are many spinners working overtime to spin every fact on its head turning and twisting it to suit their own perceived (political) ends. Everybody seems to like a good story, but nobody has the time or resources required to find out the truthfulness of its contents.

My sole purpose in going to Afghanistan was to set up this milling operation for grinding wheat and other grains available within the country, and identification of other suitable projects to be taken up later. I had never been to the country before, but had heard a lot of things about the place and the people. Some turned out to be true, some doubtful, while others were outright lies. I shall point out this fact as we go along. The book is basically a narrative as things happened and as I saw them. Any derivations or comments are based on experience and facts on the ground as seen. All people mentioned in the book are real and living, however some are now no longer with us. Mostly first names have been used wherever required except where it was necessary to identify and refer to a specific person. An effort has been made to adhere to the chronological sequence of events; however it may have been compromised at places for clarity. It is not possible to describe fully the sounds (or the absence of it) and smells of Afghanistan at that time, in writing. However, some description of it has been added where possible. Only, one who lived through it can feel and keep the experience with him, for the rest of his life.

I decided to write this book before memories become too distant and forgetfulness sets in. An honest effort has been made to state all conversations as far as I can recollect and for their relevance. It is an honest effort to bring out the true nature of things as they occurred, notwithstanding what was reported in the press. The irony of the story will be evident to most readers, and that is one of the purposes of writing this book. Separating fact from fiction is never easy, and in the case of Afghanistan it is even more so. But it is not impossible; especially if you saw it all happen first hand. The reason being that very little was known about the place before the Russian invasion. And after it was over in 1989, the world promptly forgot all about it again. It would have been much better for the country if it had stayed that way. But 9/11 changed all that. The Taleban regime was doing some good work for the people and the country within their limited capacity. It had gotten rid of warlords and brought about rule of (divine) law to a lawless society. Crime rate was almost zero including white-collar crimes. However, the sanctions imposed by UN were making the people suffer for crimes never committed or intended.

I have no idea how this book will be received when published. It is my earnest desire that a clear picture emerges after going through these pages and a balanced and informed opinion becomes easier to form and keep. During my stay in Afghanistan I found that the Taleban could be as reasonable, peace loving and gentle as anybody else although dressed in flowing robes (Shalwar & Kamize) and a turban. I could see (from my vantage point) that Mullah Omer and the Taleban were being demonized

The next meeting took place in August again at his house and proved to be fateful and very thought provoking. In this meeting 2 men from Afghanistan joined us, who were ex Mujahedeen and had fought against the Russians. They were volunteers who decided to do something for their beloved country and to provide means of livelihood for their impoverished but proud countrymen. Here is a gist of what they had to say:

- All funds belonging to Afghanistan Government deposited in Western banks had been frozen, including those of ARIANA, the Afghanistan civil airlines.
- Afghanistan was a debt free country and was free from the clutches of the well known (usual) international donors.
- They had tacit approval from Mullah Omar himself, but were meeting us here on their own initiative.
- The Government of Afghanistan will extend all and every kind of help in setting up these projects.
- We shall have a blanket approval to visit anywhere in the 95% area of the country, under Taliban control at that time.
- We would be free to pick and choose any project according to its profitability/ suitability according to our needs.
- Loans and help had been offered to Mullah Omar through intermediaries by the West with "conditions", which he refused.
- All Western concerns working in Afghanistan on various developmental projects had gone home, abandoning all works in hand at various levels of completion.
- Osama Bin Laden had contributed large sums of money to the Government's kitty to pay salaries and wages to the people working for the Government, without any conditions. Funds coming in from that source were now a trickle.

- The ordinary people of the country were now dirt poor and there was hardly any gainful employment available to them, including that provided by the Government.
- Afghanistan was in dire need of some kind of economic activity to alleviate the desperate situation developing fast.
- There were Foreign NGOs at work, but they were basically distributing food and making people dependent and subservient to them for even their basic needs.
- These NGOs could leave at the drop of a hat leaving the people high and dry, with no alternative available to them.
- They were also involved in spying and other anti state activities and the Government knew it, but had to tolerate them for want of a better option.

On hearing this woeful tale and other facts about a desperate situation in the country our hearts melted. However, we knew that a thorough examination and research was needed before proceeding further, as risks involved were enormous. The idea of a company or an NGO to undertake this perilous journey was discussed for the first time there, in my presence. Anyway it was decided that my friend Mr. Arshad and I should visit Afghanistan and see our selves what was possible and what was not. Next week after this meeting I was taken by Arshad to meet an eminent and decorated scientist of Pakistan we shall call Mr. Sultan. I found him to be a thoughtful, down to earth and humble person. He floated many ideas as to what could be done to help out a brotherly Muslim nation. He had a vision for the development of the country and was beginning to formulate concrete plans so as to bring it to fruition. My primary concern at this initial stage was the commercial viability of any undertaking. I could foresee that some people will invest in these ventures and they would then demand to see a profit. I also wanted to understand the structure of any organization set up and my role in it and how it will be funded.

A week or so after that I went with Arshad to Lahore to meet the people involved for a comprehensive and detailed discussion as to how to proceed further. All those people I met there were first and foremost a motivated lot. All were in there 50's or 60's and only had a vague idea as to what was involved. Risks were weighed against opportunities and profits etc. It was concluded that risks were very high but so were the profits. Besides, helping these unfortunate souls was a humanitarian gesture worth all the risks. Esoteric reasons held sway in the end and a go ahead was given by consensus. There was also a sense of adventure in sailing in uncharted waters.

Below are sketchy details of all those I met in Lahore:

- 1 was a retired Brigadier
- 3 were industrialists based in Lahore
- 2 were retired professional engineers
- 1 was a retired Air Force officer
- Mr. Sultan, who was the head technical honcho for a sugar mill at that time
- Mr. Arshad and myself from The Navy
- 1 was a doctor and professor of medicine

That is 11 in all. All became our shareholders later on except one of the Lahore industrialists. The idea of an organization and its naming to launch and manage this developmental activity in Afghanistan was also discussed in this meeting. Name proposed was Ummah Tameer e Nau, UTN for short. I opposed the idea saying that let it hang loose and see how things develop at first. Besides we can work together on varied projects within the Country without belonging to an organization, as long as we sort out amongst ourselves as to the role each has to play. Some supported the idea; and I later found out that in fact an

NGO type of organization by the name of UTN had indeed been formulated about 6 months back. They had been sending delegations of concerned people to Afghanistan to see for them selves the opportunities available there. It will be discussed at length later.

Now here was a totally destroyed Country of proud people who comprised mostly of hard working tribal people with traditions going back centuries. As reported in the press the infrastructure was almost totally damaged. How the people were surviving was beyond me as I had not seen it so far. This perception was about to change when I visited Afghanistan for the first time in September 2000. Arshad summarized the situation in the country for me as follows:

- The people were very friendly, forthcoming and helpful.
- Deprivation was extreme. They had so very little to go by.
- Government was however functioning and its control was evident, it was amazingly effective.
- They had a love/ hate relationship with Pakistan. Some praised the Intelligence Agencies of Pakistan for their positive contribution while others loathed them for their anti Afghan policies.
- Hate for the West was pervasive because of the sanctions imposed.
- They were suspicious of all European and American NGOs working in the Country, but were allowing them to continue for the time being, for want of a better alternative.
- We were in a position to provide that alternative by starting economic activity on a country- wide scale, honestly and quickly.

FIRST IMPRESSIONS

Arshad and I flew to Quetta in September 2000 and after an overnight stay took a cab to drive to Kandahar from Quetta. The cab took us across Chaman/ Spin Boldok border. All the unnecessary checking was on the Pakistan side and none whatsoever on the Afghan side. There were about 10 security check posts of various definitions from Quetta to Chaman. We were stopped at 2 of them and after a thorough check allowed to proceed. The border crossing was a funny site to me. All manners and kinds of people were crossing with hardly any check, no passports, no papers, nothing. However, suddenly people were stopped and checking started. When I asked around the reason for it, I was told that an officer of some department had come along on his merry rounds. This is for his consumption, so that he can report to his bosses in Quetta and Islamabad that strict control is being exercised at the border. He did not stay for more than 30 minutes, as he did not want to bother the people and hinder the smooth flow of traffic across the border. This was the norm rather than the exception on the Pakistan side. There were about 7 different departments/ agencies monitoring the border on this side. They were all there to make a quick buck if they could; no one was interested in the job at hand.

On my subsequent several crossings across this border I saw petty cash changing hands, and the guards letting go for as little as 5 rupees. There was always a rush at the border, with people crossing mostly on foot, and smaller numbers on bikes, on donkeys or donkey carts, in cars and trucks. The sight presented a chaotic scene, but it was all on purpose, so that greasing of the palms could go on unchecked. Everybody knew it but turned a blind eye, which was to mutual benefit of all concerned, those crossing and those checking. The road from Quetta to Chaman was tolerable, with potholes in some places, but otherwise passable. It was difficult to read a newspaper while being driven on this road for the most part. This will give a fairly good idea of its condition in 2000. People drove at breakneck speeds if they could, and this was like a tradition, almost. I kept telling the driver of the cab to be careful and slow down, but he couldn't care less and drove as he liked.

All kinds of daily use consumer items were going to Afghanistan from Pakistan on this vital road. Some, which I could make out, were: flour, fertilizer, sugar, tires, building material, ghee, live chicken, shoes, clothes and cloth. Trade seemed to be brisk in the border town of Chaman on the Pakistan side, where foreign goods were sold duty free (smuggled in) in the market. Most buyers came from Karachi, Quetta and Sindh in that order. Mostly scrap (steel and other metals) new and used tires were coming into Pakistan from across the border. However, the shops in Chaman were well stocked with consumer electronic items and these were surely coming from Afghanistan; but these items were not crossing over visibly. The border was normally closed after sunset and re opened around sunrise. It is possible that all contraband items were taken across, either way, during this period. During daytime the incoming traffic was less than the outgoing, and I estimated a ratio of 1 to 3 in favour of Pakistan.

Sultan saw and faced a similar situation while crossing the border at Torkhum. Once he was held up for hours by a clerk of the immigration control for no apparent reason. There is an Exit Control List (ECL) kept at the border with the immigration department. This list was being maintained to harass the people only. The list was almost never consulted except when they wanted to teach somebody a lesson or due to whimsical behaviour. It was a very hot and humid day and the clerk decided to tout his powers. He kept leafing through the perfectly legitimate passport of Sultan for a very long time asking ridiculous questions, as if to while away the time. He got exasperated and told him that a silly question begets a silly answer, so you better get on with the job at hand. That was probably the trigger he was waiting for. He told him that he was not satisfied with his *sensible* answers and called a peon to take him to the big boss for further questioning.

The *big boss* was sitting under a shady tree with friends and sipping tea. Sultan, nearly 70 years old, stood like an accused in front of this man half his age. The questions he asked were sillier than those of the clerk and Sultan's patience almost ran out. He however persevered and controlled his anger. After about 2 hours he was taken back to the same clerk and he entered all his antecedents in a register before letting him go. All this was happening when people were crossing over without passports or visas of any kind. They were waved through on payment of a paltry sum to various personnel of a coterie of agencies and departments manning the border on the Pakistan side. On crossing over everything changed. It was almost too good to be true. The officials on the Afghan side were underpaid or sometimes not paid at all. A peon on the Pakistan side was making more money than a Minister in the Afghan government, but there was no corruption. When Sultan and his colleagues told the Afghan immigration as to what they went through on the Pakistan side, they started to apologize on behalf of the Pakistani staff. They stamped their passports without asking any question and they sailed through Afghan immigration in 5 minutes.

As for myself, on crossing the border into Afghanistan from Chaman to Wesh (in Afghanistan) things started to change, slowly at first and then dramatically as we went deeper into the country. There was hardly any checking of passports or documents on the Afghan side. When we entered the immigration office, it was manned by a single man who stamped entry on our passports without asking a question. We left in 5 minutes, whereas on the Pakistan side it took us about an hour, waiting for someone to arrive to stamp exits. We took another cab from Spin Boldok for Kandahar, known as *saracha* in local dialect. The road was derelict, and at places there was no road, just tracks in dust. The cabs kicked up storms of dust as they sped past each other. The drivers drove as if they were driving sports cars on perfectly carpeted roads, and I was impressed by their skill and daring. The terrain up to Kandahar is mostly rocky with low hills or sand. One can see the vast desert stretching like a sea on the left as you drive towards Kandahar. There was only 1 check post worth the name up to the end of our journey, and they waved us on without stopping. It was a welcome change from what we saw happening in Pakistan.

In Kandahar we met the Consul General of Pakistan for a very useful and informative discussion about the way things were in this province, and elsewhere. He was a Pushtun from Sadda in Northern areas of Pakistan and had made many friends there. He told us that although Mullah Omar lives here, he allows control to be exercised from Kabul, thus we will have to go and apply in Kabul if we wanted to set up any industry in the country. The Mullah exercised moral authority more than a physical one all over the Country. People knew and saw his simple lifestyle, thus considered him as one of their own. They followed and obeyed him out of awe and respect rather than anything else. Policy was made in Kandahar and policy decisions were taken by consultation amongst about five of Mullah Omar's close advisers and the concerned Governors. Day to day running of the Government was handled by and at Kabul. We also met the Governor of Kandahar, Mullah Hasan, without any prior appointment. Just walked up to his office and found him outside talking with some other people of the area. He was an ex-Mujahid too from the Russian period and had had a leg amputated from knee down. There were no guards or security visible as far as we could see. He had a great sense of humour and a simple approach to everything, and we liked him instantly in this first meeting. He invited us for a cup of tea inside his offices and we went in together. The rooms that we saw inside the building seemed to be very large because of lack of furniture in them. His office was barely furnished too and we sat down on a carpet with round pillows (*Gao Takea*) provided to support our backs.

There was a guesthouse comprising of six rooms, by the side of the main entrance and the Governor offered us to stay in one of them for as long as we were in Kandahar. We gratefully accepted and thanked him. He said that there was no need for that, as he would accommodate even the Northern Alliance and its western supporters if they came to Kandahar as his guests. The best feature of these guest rooms were the attached baths with flushed toilets, which were rare in Kandahar in September 2000. He had been briefed about our mission and said that he had had occasion to meet others who came to see him with similar ideas but nothing came out of it. He was however an incurable optimist and welcomed all those who came to see him with open arms. He assured us that we will find no obstacles to investing in Afghanistan as compared to Pakistan, where without bribes nothing can be done. He had lived in Pakistan off and on since childhood and knew the country and its ways intimately.

He carried fond memories of the time he spent in Pakistan and narrated many interesting anecdotes about the Afghan Jihad with the Russians. One was about a four-wheel drive vehicle called *Seeh Murgh* (Ostrich), which was assembled and supplied by Iran and paid for by Pakistan, to the Mujahedeen for all kinds of arduous duties, like carrying troops and providing a movable firing platform for machine guns etc. He was apprehensive at first when he came across this vehicle and loudly protested that the Afghan forces have been deceived and coerced into accepting this sub standard vehicle by the Pakistanis and Iranians. However, once he saw it performing in actual war conditions, he had to change his mind. He told us that this amazing four wheel drive had the ability to climb out of ditches fully loaded and withstood tremendous amount of war abuse and kept running. Sadly, it is no more in production now. If there was a war museum ever built in Afghanistan this *Seeh Murgh* should occupy a place of honour in it.

Later during our stay I got a chance to visit Kandahar prison located just outside the city on the road, which goes to Heraat. I was surprised to see lack of security both inside and outside the prison. There was a separate section reserved for women and children and it was overflowing. There were no guards on duty in this section, but it was remarkably cleaner than the men's ward. On my enquiries I was told that all these women are destitute; they came here voluntarily for a meal or two for themselves and their children. The Governor has allowed them to run this section and keep it clean. No woman approaching the prison was refused. Security in the men's section was also lax, but there were never any escape attempts.

Our next stop was Kabul to meet up with Mr. Suhail, whom I met for the first time in Islamabad at Arshad's house. The road to Kabul was almost completely decimated and all bridges were destroyed. However, the intrepid drivers of this devastated road had carved out navigable routes, which passed for a road. They drove as fast as they could with Taleban songs (music without instruments) blaring from speakers within. After a while we took a liking to these haunting songs, without understanding the phrases, of course. While coming to Kandahar from Chaman, the cabbie played Hindi and Urdu songs at first, but as we neared Kandahar he switched tapes and played the allowed lyrics only. I noticed that there were well-hidden niches carved out inside the cab to hide the forbidden music tapes. There were long tangled lines of tape hung at prominent places alongside the road for every one to see and pay heed. These were the tapes caught in random roadside checking and confiscated by the Taleban. The cabbies however regularly defied the ban and learned to get away with it with practice. They got unlucky occasionally and the result was there for all to see.

The normally 6-hour journey to Kabul took about 18 hours to complete and a night-stop by the roadside was mandatory. There were no hotels or inns to stay for the night only eating places designed in such a way that these doubled as sleeping places as night fell. The arrangement was simple and basic. Food was served and eaten on rugs sitting down. These were then brushed clean at the end of the day. Curtains hung up for the day were then lowered and people slept within on the same rugs, with their bags by the side. Some spread a cloth to sleep on while others didn't. There was no danger of thievery or any fear of any crime as they slept in these open places. One can't even think of sleeping at such places in Afghanistan anymore, now that things have changed. A picture of tranquillity and peace along these roads has been torn apart. There was plenty of local food available at all times, however items imported from outside (mostly Pakistan) were scarce at times. But Iranian stuff was everywhere and in plentiful quantities, which was a welcome relief. Fruit was in abundance and apples, pomegranates; *garma/ sarda* (a kind of large melon) and grapes were of the finest quality and inexpensive. We bought some apples, grown near Ghazni from a roadside fruit shop and took them with us to Kabul. Their pleasant fragrance filled the car all along the way and our rooms where we stayed.

There were roadside motor workshops manned by highly skilled mechanics and technicians along the way. They seemed to perform miracles with just basic tools. The business was brisk under the prevailing road conditions and the driving speeds in practice. We experienced breakdowns too in our various travels to and forth on this road. Every time the skill of these men amazed me. It was obvious that they had honed their skills with constant practice and hard work. It seems that same skills and practice are being used now so effectively to design and manufacture Improvised Explosive Devices (IED's) for use along these and other roads. We encountered a remarkable amount of camaraderie and goodwill while travelling on these dilapidated roads. We met complete strangers on the way and sat down to eat, sleep and discuss the future together over several cups of black or green tea. I noticed that optimism was more common than a pessimistic outlook in spite of the prevailing circumstances. There is something about the Afghan Spirit which foreigners not familiar with the place and its people will find very hard to understand. They believed in destiny to the extent that they had resigned themselves to its consequences. This belief brought about a strange and pervasive contentment, which we had not seen in any people before, anywhere.

On reaching Kabul for the first time, I was struck by the amount of destruction all around. Hardly any building seemed intact. They were all either completely destroyed or partially damaged. But people were living in them for want of a better alternative. It was a pathetic and depressing sight and I remember cursing out loud for those responsible for this state of affairs. Mr. Suhail met us at the cab station and he took us to his house in Wazir Akbar Khan Colony. The house was abandoned property and he was living in it for the time being. Very quickly we noticed that he had no money to keep us at his house for any length of time, but he insisted that we go with him out of traditional Pushtun hospitality. We then forced him to accept a contribution from us for our period of stay, otherwise we shall leave. He relented with great difficulty. That was an experience well learned and just in time, as we were bound to face similar situations subsequently. It gives a measure of urban poverty prevalent in the country at that time. The main reason was that there was no gainful employment available in Kabul or elsewhere to make both ends meet.

Next day we went to see some senior officials and ministers in the Government with Suhail on hand. Everywhere we had to drink the traditional Afghan tea (*qahwa*) and were welcomed with open arms. There was no protocol to go by, no security checks, no doormen or ushers. All the doors and windows of the offices were open, most had no curtains or were drawn apart, if they had them. Discussion was frank and to the point. They wanted us to start some economic activity as early as possible at our terms. I was impressed by the level of their concern for the general public and absence of any desire to generate funds for the Government in the form of taxes/ duties/ licenses and what have you. I noticed very little paper being pushed or used. People just walked in with a single sheet of paper and the job was done there and then by the officer. He scribbled something with a pencil on the same paper or a chit kept by him, and that was it. People left happy, smiling and satisfied. It was gratifying to look at their faces as they left free of anxiety or tension. What a sea change as compared to Pakistan, just across the border. It was obvious that most of the problems faced by common people on a daily basis in Pakistan were because of this lack of concern for their well being by officialdom there. Comparisons made things more clear and a stark difference in approach of these Afghan officials was evident. The interaction between the Ministers, Officers and Subordinate staff was remarkable. It was so informal, frank and above board that it surprised us. We contemplated and discussed amongst ourselves this remarkable atmosphere of understanding and smooth functioning in all the ministries that we visited.

Next day, all 3 of us went for a survey of the markets, and found that almost all goods being sold were imported from Pakistan, Iran or the bordering Central Asian countries. Merchandise from Pakistan was most abundant, and consisted of daily use items mostly. The markets were bustling with people and pricing was very competitive, which was good for the shoppers. There were women shopping freely, most were burqa- clad, however others just used a sheet (chadder) to cover themselves. We noticed that some were wearing baggy pants under the covering and nobody seemed to bother. There were many Sikh and Hindu merchants in the market doing business side by side their Muslim compatriots. We noticed very little or no police, traffic or otherwise, on the roads. There were no roadblocks or security checking of any kind in the city worth mentioning. Begging was common, mostly by women and children, whose husbands or fathers had been killed or disabled in the long war.

We bought an old SUV from Kandahar for travelling at a throwaway price. I took this vehicle to town in Kabul to replace its hydraulic shock absorbers. It was a lengthy job and I sat down by the pavement on a stool provided by the mechanic's assistant. After about an hour a young woman in her early thirties with a child about 3 or 4 years in tow came and sat down on the pavement near where I was sitting. She kept quiet for some time, but as soon as the mechanic was out of hearing range started talking. I could make out the gist of what she was saying as she spoke in Persian mostly, which I can just about understand if spoken clearly. She seemed to be educated and spoke quite clearly. The child was her offspring from a husband killed in the war, as were all her brothers and father. There was no male member of the family left. She was thus destitute and desperate and said that she will go with me to wherever I wanted to take her as a slave for life. All she asked in return was just enough to feed her and her child. I tried not to pay too much attention, but had to swallow hard several times during her disjointed discourse, as she used to stop abruptly when somebody was within earshot. Although she was wearing a *burqa,* her face was not hidden and desperation was written all over it.

We later found out that there were not enough police uniforms to go by, for the policemen on duty. Thus some stayed home or worked elsewhere to make ends meet. However some came for duty in civvies and performed well. We were told over and over again that the need to rehabilitate the helpless dependants of those who sacrificed their lives for their country was priority number one for the Government. There was no money to do that, thus a bad situation had become worse, hence the begging. We also met some foreigners, mostly Arabs who had married locally and settled down in Kabul. They contributed in cash and kind to help out as much as they could. It was remarkable how quickly they had adapted to a very different traditional culture prevalent in Afghanistan. They seemed well settled and satisfied with their predicament, notwithstanding the daily encumbrances that life presented in Kabul at that time.

We also visited Ghazni about 100 Km from Kabul. There was the mausoleum of Mahmud Ghaznavi there, standing amidst tall shady trees. One felt a strange kind of peace, being there. The caretaker showed us an ancient key and padlock made in India from the times of his conquests. We sat down to have lunch in one of biggish café in the market place and made some interesting discoveries during the course of the meal. Ghazni was the biggest animal market in the Country, and all kinds of animals were brought here for slaughter and trading. All hides and skins went out to Pakistan in raw form with only rudimentary treatment for the long journey. This resulted in a lot of them being wasted en route, reaching almost rotten, thus fetching a very low price. There was also wheat flour bags brought in from Pakistan by way of Parachinar/ Khost border; specially, when the normal route (Torkhum/ Landikotal border) was closed for any reason. From here it was dispatched in trucks to Southern parts of the Country. It was a sort of hub for goods coming from the north, west and east of the Country and being sent south.

In Kabul we met a colourful and interesting individual, who was originally from Pakistan. He had now settled in Afghanistan with all his 4 wives, 2 of them from Pakistan. He was a great advocate for keeping multiple wives, and recounted its virtues at the drop of a hat. He retired from Pakistan Air Force as a Flight Lieutenant in Logistics. He accompanied us back to Kandahar, where he was now living, and put us up in his large house in the outskirts of the city. We were very grateful for that because there was no place worth the name to stay there. He was thinking of establishing a small milling operation (grinding wheat) to produce the most common- use staple i.e. flour (*atta or urro in local dialect*). That got us thinking and we visited the destroyed wheat silos and mill constructed by Italians in Arghandab area, north of the city. We found it to be operable but at a very high cost, because all machinery was of Italian origin with some parts missing and some damaged beyond repair. Its throughput was also not very impressive as it was designed in Italy for Italian markets, then transported to Kandahar for installation here. It was a common mistake we were to see later over and over again in all industries installed in Afghanistan in the public sector. Most such projects installed with foreign collaboration did not take the local conditions into consideration resulting in waste of limited resources. A new flourmill with Pakistan designed machinery was feasible and easier to install. Such a mill was more suited to local conditions, because of its high throughput, easier maintenance and availability of common spares locally.

In June 2001 Sultan asked Mr. Tayyab, political secretary to Mullah Omar to allow filming in Kabul and elsewhere by a TV crew he took along with him from Pakistan. He wanted to negate the vicious propaganda campaign launched by the western media and show the true picture to the world at large. His request was declined by Mr. Agha, warning him that punishment for the offense of filming was 3 months jail. Sultan then requested Mullah Hasan, the Governor of Kandahar, explaining to him the dire need to show the world the real situation on ground. This would go a long way in attracting investment to Afghanistan, he told him. That convinced him and he recorded an illuminating and lucid 2 hour interview from 10 to 12 pm at night the next day. He then got permission to film inside Kandahar city and its environs. This was done and it is a permanent record on film about how effective was the ban on poppy cultivation and processing. Ordinary people freely expressed their opinions on film without fear or favour, an amazing display of freedom of speech. This is, believe it or not, absolutely true. Next, this team went to Kabul and was allowed to record on film restoration of electric power to the city from broken down and dilapidated transmission and distribution system, inherited by Taleban after years of neglect, without spares and any outside help. They were then taken in tow by the ministry of information and recorded 7 hours of video in and around Kabul. This was probably the first attempt by anybody to show the world real face of Taleban and ground realities in Afghanistan.

The fact is that Taleban never considered it necessary to negate the falsehoods being spread against them by the western press. Small and insignificant omissions or mistakes by the Taleban were stretched and shown as monumental failures and successes were being simply ignored. When this sate of affaires was discussed with them by us, they said that we are doing, whatever we are doing, for Allah only. So it does not matter to us. But we emphasized that this approach is not correct, the world must be told the truth if nothing else. People of the world were not fools (cannot say that for the governments) and it was their right to see the true picture. Lies being spread, such as the Taleban are extremists, violence prone, against progress, opposed to women education, illiterate, unaware of governance theories and management techniques in a modern world, must be negated. None of it was true and we are witness to that.

This was discussed with Mullah Zaif, the Afghan ambassador in Islamabad and he agreed to go along with us. As a result Sultan was able to take along with him a Japanese born Filipino journalist to Afghanistan in one of his trips at about the same time. He was briefed about Afghan history, geography and culture in Islamabad, before embarking on the trip. He stayed there for about a month and travelled extensively. On return, he told us that he had lot of misgivings and misconceptions about the country, which have all been washed away. He went back and wrote a convincing first hand report, debunking western propaganda about Afghanistan in July 2001. Another offshoot was that a Hong Kong based commercial television crew of three agreed gladly, to accompany the UTN delegation to Kabul and Kandahar in the month of August 2001.

Taxi was the preferred mode of transport in Kabul like other urban centres. These were cheap and available everywhere. We saw buses plying in the city also. But these were reserved for women and children only. Men were not allowed to board because there were not enough of them available. Many women had lost their men folk in the on going turmoil for the last 30 years. Thus they were compensated and facilitated by the authorities by providing these buses, which charged nominal fare. Taxi fare was also half that of Pakistan and all kinds of motor transport was abundantly available at one-third the rates in Pakistan. Roads and roundabouts inside the city were constantly being improved and we saw significant degree of improvement in 6 months time. Reconstruction seemed to be the priority number one of the Government. Not much attention was being paid to the military build up, which was required considering the situation at that time.

When the Taleban took over Kabul, it was a destroyed city. There was no electricity, pot holed roads, no hospitals, no schools and gutted market areas. People lived in a constant state of fear day and night. All activity ceased by sunset and did not get underway well after sunrise. People could not go to sleep even after locking themselves in. This situation prevailed in all cities, towns and villages without exception. In 5 years they had repaired most roads within the city, schools for boys and girls were functioning, hospitals were open late into the night, markets were bustling and the same people now left their houses and shops unlocked when they went out. One could sleep under a tree in a park without fear of molestation. There was no theft or robbery worth mentioning anywhere in the 95% area of the country under Taleban control. Opium production ceased, all unauthorized arms and ammunition had been confiscated and disrupted electric power had been restored in most of the country.

During and after these initial visits to Afghanistan I came away with the impression that there was minimal government there. As President Ronald Reagan once said, "Government is not the solution to our problem, government is the problem". That is why Thomas Jefferson (one of the founding fathers of United States) was in favour of a limited government, because it governs the least.[2] It does not extort money from the people in the name of this or that tax, thus forcing them to evade taxes. Also it is not in the habit of declaring a thing or an act illegal in the name of propriety, morality, equality or welfare of the poor forcing them to resort to impropriety, immorality[3] etc. I could see

---

[2] Khalil Ahmad, *Tax Evasion and Money Laundering in Pakistan: An Overview.* Alternate Solutions Institute, Lahore. August, 2004. **www.hum-azad.org**
[3] Ibid.

that the laws enacted and promulgated were quite flexible in a collective sense, where the government was involved. People were absolutely free to transact business within the country amongst themselves or with foreigners. The laws were severe only where life, honour or property of a citizen was at stake.

GETTING TO WORK

Arshad and I came back to Islamabad towards the end of September 2000. We briefed Sultan and all others on hand and it was decided to start the first real venture in Afghanistan in the form of a series of flourmills at Kandahar, Kabul, Mazar e Sharif, Herat, Ghazni and Jalalabad, in that order. An application to that effect was lodged by Suhail in Kabul right away and approval was given in the 4th week of October, 2000. Kandahar was to be the first to get a large flourmill up and running. Drive for funds started in earnest and Sultan used all his influence and acumen to convince people to contribute or invest in this venture for religious and humanitarian reasons. My job was to highlight the commercial viability and profitability of the projects in hand. This was not difficult, as we had enough data, statistical and otherwise to convince them. It was a question of putting two and two together and clear enough pictures emerged for people to see and understand. We were surprised at the overwhelming response we got from sympathetic and good at heart sort of people from Pakistan and abroad. The people saw and felt the injustice of it all: the richest nations of the world bent upon destroying the poorest. This feeling and understanding was at the root of all contributions that we received; it was a worldwide phenomenon, we found. It was amazing to find the deep understanding (which clear thinking brings) around the world, about the real situation in Afghanistan. People were not being duped after all by all those falsehoods being churned out by the mainstream media in the West. For all intent and purposes this understanding is still there, if somebody taps into it, he may be able to bring some sanity to this region.

Most of our investors, who became shareholders later, were retired from senior Government positions after superannuation. Some were entrepreneurs and venture capitalists, if one can call them that. All felt satisfied contributing and participating in a worthy cause. They knew the risks involved but said that their money will be well spent in helping the ones most in need. They were not overly worried about loss or profit in a commercial sense, and felt a kind of joy (of gratefulness) when parting with their money. This was heart-warming and a little surprising to me but I felt a huge responsibility and a burden to see through the trust reposed in us by these God fearing people. Of course, like everybody else we could not foresee 9/11 happening in 2001, in October 2000. But it happened and changed everything, ruining so many lives and laying waste all the meticulous planning we had done to undertake an economic activity to rid the people of overbearing poverty in Afghanistan.

After the approval for milling operations the work actually started on Kandahar flourmill in November 2000, more about that later. But first a glimpse of all the hard work and planning which was put in to identify and undertake about fifty different projects, on a countrywide scale. From the outset in late 1999 when this idea of starting economic activity in Afghanistan started to take shape, an effort was undertaken to survey and mark the projects, which were most feasible, urgently needed and easier to start. Towards that end several visits were undertaken by professional engineers, doctors, professors and businessmen to see the ground reality for them. These visits proved very fruitful and a detailed list of feasible projects was drawn up as a result of this survey. I participated in this effort from September 2000 onwards and saw many destroyed industries, factories and farms, which could be restored and set to work. The Government told us to lay down our own terms to do this and they accepted all our submissions. Basically we told them that we had an obligation towards our investors to give them a fair return on their investment (ROI), before we hand back any completed project. Most undertakings were to be run on Build, Operate, Own and Transfer (BOOT) basis, but with no time limits of any kind set by them on us, giving us a free hand in management and operations. The concerned authorities trusted us to deliver and were satisfied by all the presentations that we made. At no stage there was ever any talk of commissions or kickbacks. What a relief it was; it is difficult to describe in words.

Below is a list of the projects surveyed to be undertaken. It will give an idea of the scale of development effort planned for the uplift of the country, the so-called capacity building:

1.   **Re-melting of Scrap and re-rolling mills**: Plenty of scrap was available within the country. There was a huge demand for building materials, which this mill would produce. Locations were also worked out for ease of supply and transportation etc. One such operation was set up by a Karachi based entrepreneur near where our flourmill later came up. He had to leave and go back to Karachi because of some family issues, promising to return as soon as he could. But then the attack came and government changed; he then decided to stay back in Karachi.

2.   **Rehabilitation of Combined Cycle Electric Power Plant and Power Supply System:** This was in Kabul. It was being set up by Brown Bovary (or BBC, at that time) from Switzerland. They left it about 80% complete, but without any trials. They apparently were planning to come back, as we found all parts, and some more, required for the 20% incomplete portion. They most probably left in a hurry; the signs were everywhere.

3.   **Coal Fired Electric Power Plants**: Very good quality coal was available at Pul-e- Charkhi and other places throughout the Country. Herat coal was of exceptional quality. There was a closed working mine there, which was being managed by Czechoslovakian engineers before shut down.

4.   **Iron Ore and Steel Making Plant**: Naturally occurring iron ore was easily extractable and of very

high quality. The ore contains 62% iron, which is very high and rare worldwide.

5. **Coal Mining and Coke making Plants**: China was/is a large market for good quality coke. Pakistan also buys coke from abroad at a very high price for steel making. Coke made in Afghanistan could satisfy needs of both the countries.

6. **Oil and Gas wells—Crude production and Oil Refinery project:** Such good quality crude was available that it went into trucks almost directly from the ground. The only treatment being given was large round containers underneath which log and crude fires were lighted. Fuel was siphoned off the top into trucks. It was a scene worth watching. 12 producing wells had been dug along the Uzbek and Tajik borders by German and Russian engineers. All were shut down (capped) because of lack of working capital and skilled manpower.

7. **Rare Earths and Purification Plants:** There is a mountain about 9 by 6 Km in Helmand province which consists almost entirely of rare earths (besides Lithium, Gold and Copper) used in rocketry and electronics etc. The area is called Khan Nasheen and Dr. Chaudhry (UTN's Director Engineering) paid a visit to it and submitted a positive report. However, the need was acutely felt for a wide-ranging mineral-testing laboratory to proceed further. Plans for a laboratory were on the anvil when situation changed for the worse.

8. **Water Works/ Hydro Power Plants and Irrigation Dams for Extraction of Copper, Gold and Silver**: Copper, gold, silver and other metals in abundance in very remote areas, where no water or power was available. Second largest deposit of copper in the world is in Kuner province. It is of exceptional quality. There were some abandoned small hydro power projects also, which could be revived and power generated for such projects

besides other uses. Gichiki Dam built on Arghandab River was producing 30 megawatts for the needs of Kandahar city. This could easily be increased to 120 by raising the height 10 meters. Plus water for irrigation would become available as a bonus. Heads of 2 Pakistani companies, FW Engineering and International Fabrication saw and discussed the project with the Minister of Water and Power. He was pleased to approve it and gave the go ahead. Chinese engineers also had a look at it and agreed to do the project at 3 times the cost projected by UTN with 50% advance in cash.

9. **Fruit Preservation and Packing Plants:** Olive gardens with irrigation systems were planted near Jalalabad on about 5000 Acres with extraction and packing plants within them. These were now all damaged and in- operable, but could be restored. The plants were of Russian origin.

10. **Cement Plants:** These were very feasible and could be ideally located near hills for raw material. One site outside Kandahar had been surveyed and the report was available in Kabul. One plant was working in Pul-e Khumri near Kabul, but at low capacity. It could be restored to full production by small additions and alterations.

11. **Textile Mills**: Damaged mills in Kabul and Kandahar could be restored easily. These were set up in the public sector during Dawood's tenure as the head of Government of Afghanistan.

12. **Mineral Development and Refining Mills:** Vey high quality mica, graphite and other minerals were easily extractable at a low cost. In Kandahar we met two Pakistani businessmen who were importing Fluoride and Chromate from mines near Kandahar into Pakistan. They were in the office of the Director General of mines and Industries based in Kandahar, looking after the mineral resources of the provinces of Kandahar, Zabul, Heraat, Helmand, Farah and

Qallat. Their agreement had expired and wanted to renew it. It took about 15 minutes for the renewal, while we were sitting there in his office. Director Engineering of UTN, Dr. Chaudhry who was there with us, commented that he applied for a share in a coalmine operation in Pakistan 2 years ago. The approval has not been given so far. He said I now know how long it takes to get such approvals in a corruption free environment: 15 minutes!

13. **Infra Structure Projects – Roads and high ways**: All existing but destroyed infrastructure was the priority. These were to be built with local and Pakistani expertise only. Some concerns in Pakistan were very interested because of a corruption free environment in Afghanistan.

14. **Marble and Onyx Industries:** We saw a white marble mountain range north of Kandahar and onyx extraction in Helmand near Pakistani border by wasteful blasting method. Afghan Green, a world famous onyx was being taken across the border to Pakistan cheaply. There was an Italian installed marble/ onyx factory in Lashkar Gah with German and Italian machines lying damaged and abandoned.

15. **Engineering Fabrication & Manufacturing Workshops:** These were planned to be set up in or near urban centres for obvious reasons. A member of UTN Engineer Yousuf had his own going concern on Bund road in Lahore. He was to take the lead in this venture.

16. **Communication networks:** There was a dire need for these as no countrywide telephone communication landlines existed. There were some small local networks only. Chinese had taken the lead in this field and they had established a 12,000 lines telephone exchange in Kabul and 8000 lines one in Kandahar. They also had set up a mobile phone company in the country and were

monopolizing the mobile phone market. Both these projects were carried by UTN to PTCL and Pak Data Com authorities in Islamabad with letters of approval from the concerned Minister. But they declined without assigning any reason.

17. **Agriculture Farms—Agro based Industries:** This venture had a very promising prospect because the Government was keen on this, and very useful input was provided by the able Minister of Water and Power. Since the country is mountainous only 22% is cultivable. Out of this only 2% was under cultivation and this could easily be increased to 10%. Tube wells and agricultural machinery/ implements were required mainly, to do the job. One promising project on which preliminary work was started by UTN was located just outside Kandahar on Heraat road. A company comprising of American, Indian and Afghani experts conducted first survey of this area in 1975. They found ample water for irrigation at a depth of 80 to 100 meters, which was being replenished by nearby Arghandab River and snowmelt from high mountains to the North. A 25 kilometre long strip along Heraat road was allocated to UTN, which measured around 12,500 acres. The plan was to develop this for cultivation and make model villages every 5 kilometres with their own dispensary, school, market etc. This was a 3 million dollar project at that time to be completed in about 3 years. Another 5-acre piece of land nearby, allotted to us, was earmarked for tissue culture.

18. **Fertilizer Plants:** These were planned with collaboration from Pakistan. Interested parties with requisite expertise were involved and termed it feasible. A large facility installed in Mazar e Sharif was selected for extensive repairs and modernization.

19. **Hardware Stores/ Manufacturing:** Required urgently for building activity going on privately and in the public domain.
20. **Vegetable Ghee Plants:** We visited 2 such plants, one in Kabul and the other west of Kandahar on Herat road. Both had damaged buildings but machinery was intact.
21. **Flour Mills and Roti Plants:** One such large Russian undertaking was in- operative due to defects and aging. It was to be revived and a series of new flour mills were planned country wide. One at Kandahar had been installed and running when deteriorating security situation forced its closing after the attack in December, 2001.
22. **Plastic Moulding Industry:** These were installed but damaged and could be revived without much investment. It was based in Kabul industrial area.
23. **Pharmaceutical Industry:** Belatedly a lot of interest was shown by Pakistani concerns in this, because of a huge demand. Initially this industry did not respond to our pleas for an urgent need to set up manufacturing units in Afghanistan. The demand was being met with imports from Iran and Pakistan at a steep cost.
24. **Galvanized Iron Pipe Mills:** Pakistani concerns were interested in setting up this important industry. They could see the potential and substantial profits after surveys conducted by us.
25. **Hotels and Restaurants:** These were needed as development activity took off and people travelled there for work etc. Local partners and investors were also interested in this sector. There used to be good functional hotels in Kandahar in the past, before the Russian invasion. These were all destroyed or damaged now. As more and more foreigners were heading towards Kandahar, since it was now the de facto capital of the country, this need for some good quality hotels had multiplied manifold. We saw at

least two large hotels in the city, both damaged and uninhabited; but their layout and location testified to glorious days gone by. Need for some good quality restaurants were also acute. Afghan cuisine begins and ends with red meat, which is sometimes too overwhelming for unfamiliar palates. Again there were local partners willing to share in such ventures. Another area we studied was the need for bakeries in all-urban centres. There were some small enterprises, but these were too basic and limited in scope and output. All those people who had been to Pakistan missed our bakery products the most and longed for them. Thus there was a readymade market waiting to be tapped.

26. **Glass Industry:** There was none in the Country, but was required as early as possible. Some Arab and Iranian entrepreneurs were taking an interest in this.

27. **Agriculture Implements Workshops:** These were required for repair and maintenance at first. Could develop into manufacturing units with time. Only crude basic repairs were possible at that time and even may be now.

28. **Water Pumps/ Motors manufacturing:** None available within the Country at that time. It was to be established in Kabul to cater for the whole Country.

29. **Tanneries—Leather making & Processing Units**: Raw hides were being sent to Pakistan with rudimentary treatment, resulting in huge losses to the Country. This was a very lucrative undertaking, thus it was one of the first to be surveyed and have its report completed. It was to be located in Mazar-e-Sharif. Site had been selected.

30. **LPG Storage and Transport System:** LPG was being brought in tankers from Turkmenistan and stored in Kandahar in a small privately owned enterprise. Demand outstripped supply all the year round. Situation was almost the same everywhere. This was to be addressed by establishing medium to

large storage units at carefully selected sites throughout the country.

31. **Manufacturing Spare Parts for Cars and Trucks:** None existed in the Country. However a huge demand was there. Used cars, buses and trucks were coming in droves from Dubai through Iran as there was only a 2% duty imposed on these. There were large showrooms for all sorts of vehicles in Herat and Kandahar. There were no restrictions on import of these vehicles.

32. **Engine Oil Blending Plant:** These were to be established after local crude oil became available for refining and marketing.

33. **Manufacture of Electrical Fittings:** Household and commercial/ industrial fittings were required throughout the Country. All were being imported at a high cost at that time.

34. **Grinding and Powdering ores/ Talcum Mills:** There was a huge demand because of weather conditions in Afghanistan. Only 1 or 2 small units existed which had become unserviceable, and were abandoned.

35. **Gemstone Mining and Cutting Industry:** There were un-exploited mines of precious and semi precious stones in Uruzgan, Khost, Nangarhar and some other provinces. The raw stones we saw were of exceptionally high quality. Ministry of Mines & Industries had some samples, which were kept in an open shelf in the Minister's office. Some people who discovered those precious stone mines in far-flung remote areas had provided these.

36. **Paper Products Manufacturing:** None existed at that time, but was required. It was planned to be taken up later, after more urgent projects were completed.

37. **Printing Presses:** Old and damaged ones were there, being run on a day-to-day basis. These were

required and easily installable in all urban centres. Not a large investment but with a large return (ROI).

38. **Soap and Soapy products manufacturing:** There were abandoned and slightly damaged units lying idle due to lack of working capital. We were handed over two of these units for running as we deemed fit.

39. **Oxygen and Industrial Gases:** None existed. This could be installed in the industrial park in Kabul, where an abandoned and empty factory building was to be handed over to us shortly.

40. **Consumer Item Factories:** A Safety match making factory was to be installed in the industrial park in Kandahar. Machinery for it was taken to Kandahar from Pakistan. Mixing industry for paints was studied and found feasible. One paint manufacturer from Pakistan visited the site and took a lot of interest in this venture.

41. **Repair of Educational/ Vocational Centres:** Colleges, Universities and other such institutions were selectively targeted and destroyed during the lawless period of the warlords, before the Taleban took control. Kabul Polytechnic Institute was selected for rehabilitation. It used to have 2500 students, 150 teachers and classes in all trades when it was functional. Besides Kabul University was probably the only university in the world providing full boarding and lodging to resident students free of cost. It had 30,000 students enrolled when working at full strength. It was a skeleton of its past now, because of lack of funds and faculty.

42. **Fibre Optic Network:** Fibre Optic network of Pak Telecom has reached Peshawar and Central Asian States to the North of Afghanistan had it too. Thus if these 2 networks were connected by installing one in Afghanistan the circle will be completed and all traffic (worldwide) will pass through Pakistan as indeed Afghanistan. This will be a good source of perpetual income for both the countries. At the moment the

system is broken as there was no FO network in Afghanistan. The concerned Minister agreed to allow Pakistan access throughout the country if we installed this network and completed the circle. A Letter of Intent was issued by the Minister of Communications and handed over to us. All equipment for this project is manufactured in Pakistan.

43. **Weighbridges:** First weighbridge was planned to be installed in Kandahar at the flourmill premises. A reputable Pakistani Karachi based company Messrs Akhtar Brothers Electro Enterprises was selected for this installation. Subsequent installations were scheduled for customs authorities in Kandahar and Kabul. Other cities were on hold to be visited later by us to assess the situation there.

44. **Development Bank:** A development bank (Islamic banking, Shariah pliant) to channel and invest funds on a countrywide basis was studied and approved. First report had been published after extensive discussions with Afghan Authorities. The bank was named Da Ummah Development Bank and it had board members from Pakistan and Afghanistan on its panel.

45. **Khost Water Supply System:** This was surveyed in March 2001 for restoration to its original capacity and some more. The system was installed by German engineers in early seventies. It had been vandalized and uprooted at places. The whole system could be modernized and upgraded to meet the requirements of Khost for up to 2025.

46. **Fertilizer Plant Restoration:** This Urea fertilizer plant was located near Mazar e Sharif. It was only partially functional at low capacity and required balancing, modernization and repairs (BMR). UTN was exploring avenues for generation of adequate funds to undertake this important project.

Reading through the list above it becomes obvious that it was all about capacity building. It was for the good of the general populace and had nothing to do with propping up the Taleban regime per se. Any benefits accruing from this kind of planning and undertaking would have gone a long way in turning these poor people away from militancy. Extreme deprivation and demeaning poverty were fuelling militancy and adoption of violent means by otherwise peaceful citizens. The Government never asked us to set up any entity to manufacture weapons of any kind, because they knew that we would refuse. Work needs to be done on the same lines today in Afghanistan without politicizing it unnecessarily. We were in a position to plan and implement what has been projected above because of zero corruption and no red tape.

We could see how orders given orally by officials at all levels were respected and obeyed. But this did not satisfy us and at times, we insisted that some kind of a document must be there for the record, the officials smiled and obliged, to satisfy us. There was a remarkable amount of trust reposed by Government officials in their day-to-day dealings with the people and vice versa. Surprisingly the people or the officials of State, saving a lot of time and hassle, making life easier for everybody, almost never abused this trust. I quote two examples below to illustrate this point of view:

a)   Cigarettes were forbidden throughout Afghanistan by February 2000. It came about after it was decided by Mullah Omar that these were harmful to health and a source of waste of money by the general public, as all cigarettes were imported from outside. We did not see anybody smoking in public after that, throughout the country.

b)   The Taleban disallowed all arms, large and small soon after coming to power. This was a country where almost everybody was armed and had been for centuries. Men wore arms as ornaments. But it all changed with just one rule made and promulgated by the Government; Afghanistan became a weapons free country almost overnight. Suhail, the man charged with taking all weapons from the people, told us that people felt ashamed giving up arms in broad daylight, so he parked open trucks at strategic locations as night fell for people to deposit their arms during night-time. Trucks were full at daybreak and all arms were taken from the people within a few weeks.

In March of 2001 the opium production in Afghanistan came down to zero. I had seen the opium bazaar of Kandahar once and it presented a bustling scene on any day of the week. But on that day there was not a soul to be seen there. It was talk of the town and people were impressed by this achievement of the regime. This became possible only after Mullah Omar decided to show the moral authority he exercised all over Afghanistan to the world. It was a difficult decision, and was taken after a lot of protracted negotiations and consultations. It took away the only source of earning from a large section of rural society, who had no alternative available to them, immediately after ceasing poppy cultivation. The final decision was delayed by months because of these agonizing negotiations. All that talk about cutting off of hands and capital punishments to achieve zero opium production is an outright lie and an attempt to malign the Taleban and undermine this remarkable achievement. It was done to show the whole world that impossibility had now become possible in such a short time. And there were a number of other possibilities knocking at the door, which were achievable, with the present set up; but nobody opened that door.

All that was required was an order passed down the line, broadcast on radio and published in local newspapers. That was it and all opium production stopped. There were a few delinquents, they were warned of dire consequences and put in jail for short periods. That did the trick and zero opium production was achieved for the first time in the history of the Country. There was a big time trader from Iranian Baluchistan who bought land the size of a city near Kandahar and settled there. He ran electric distribution lines and made roads to connect this property with the main road on his own. I helped him plan and lay electrification lines for power distribution within his city. He had fallen out with the Iranian border police and law enforcement agencies in Iran, where he lived, about 2 years ago. This property of his was about 10 Km away from our premises. He made water holes and planted trees and grass to make a large picnicking area and invited us there. He had intimate knowledge of what was going on in the poppy growing fields of Afghanistan and talked openly about it. He looked and talked like a seasoned businessman and was weary of the drug trade. He wanted the Taleban regime to eradicate it for good and set up legitimate business enterprises like the one we were developing. He took a lot of interest in our activities in the country and asked searching questions.

"This economic activity thing is probably the best way to curb crime and violence", he said while talking to me. If only this could be understood and implemented by all concerned, peace will get a chance to succeed. This Balochi fellow was hiding from Iranian authorities for fear of his life. He requested for a full pardon from the authorities in Iran, but was refused. He came to Afghanistan and pleaded with the Governor of Kandahar to give him asylum. He assured him that he will abide by the law as long as he was in Afghanistan and his province. He deposited a surety bond in the state bank as bail, and his request was granted. He lived in Afghanistan for about 2 years and then went back to Quetta in Pakistan where he had a house. Shortly after that we heard that Iranian agents in their sleep in the same house assassinated him, along with his wife. There is no doubt that he had reformed himself and was truly repentant. But he was destined to die like that, and could not run away from fate.

At the beginning of 2001 it was proposed to set up mobile hospitals based in Kabul and Kandahar to provide sorely needed medical aid in rural areas nearby. Two minibuses were purchased for this purpose, one in Kabul and one in Islamabad. The plan was to retrofit both these vehicles in Lahore and take them to Afghanistan, subsequently. However, up until October 2001 necessary permission from (indecisive) Govt. of Pakistan was not obtained. One minibus coaster was purchased in Kabul because of very low cost. But GOP did not allow it to be brought into Pakistan for outfitting, as no bribes were forthcoming from us. The one purchased in Islamabad (duty free) by Mullah Zaif, the Afghan ambassador, was also not allowed to cross over to Afghanistan, for similar reasons. Mr. Rehan was funding one hospital, a U.K based philanthropist and the other by Karachi based Feroza Hashim Foundation. This foundation was well known and working on many educational and medical projects in Pakistan and Bangladesh. We learned quite a few lessons about the psyche of our bureaucratic set up doing this project. The most important being the timid self serving nature of the civilian bureaucracy.

After extended discussions here in Pakistan and later in Afghanistan it was decided to launch schemes to rehabilitate widows and orphans, who had nowhere to go and nobody to turn to. For this small carpet making looms were earmarked to be supplied to the deserving families door to door. These looms were priced at about 8 to 10,000 Rupees at that time. Large ones cost about 25,000. It was projected that in about 15 to 20,000 Rupees an average sized (5 persons) family could be rehabilitated. Some of these families were being provided with bread by NGO's, standing in long lines all day. This eroded their self-esteem and the will to survive under adverse circumstances. If they could make a living by their own hands it would go a long way in ameliorating the despondency which we saw setting in. These handloom carpets were to be marketed worldwide by manufacturers/ exporters from Pakistan, who were keen to help with cash and kind in this venture. Another project on similar lines was to manufacture footballs and volleyballs for the local and international market. Some manufacturers in Sialkot (centre of sports industry in Pakistan) agreed to provide material and knowhow for this scheme. It was feasible because this is a labour intensive industry and labour rates were low in Afghanistan. Initial marketing was proposed to be local, graduating to international as skills developed. Third option was embroidery and knitting work for which female hands were most suited. Some entrepreneurs in Pakistan were interested and agreed to provide all help in setting up these centres in Kabul initially, expanding to other cities with time. An office was also opened in Kabul by UTN for such and similar projects.

A number of surveys of educational institutions in and around Kabul were conducted from January to July 2001. The condition of all these institutions was heart rending. There were no doors or windows left. All glass was broken; water pipes and taps had been ripped apart and masonry was pock marked with bullet and shrapnel holes. Students were sitting on bare floors and walls were blackened to use as blackboards. For example Habibia College used to be an elitist institution in the times of king Zahir Shah. It had 5000 students on its rolls in its 3 storey high grand building built by the Americans. It now had 100 students, no light and no water. The sight it presented was pathetic. Sheikh Hashim of Feroza Hashim Foundation announced a donation of 25 lakh Rupees on the spot on seeing it. He was visibly moved as we walked through the devastated building. However it was estimated that one crore and 25 lakh was required for its restoration. An effort was launched by UTN for these funds and people were responding positively. We then called on the Minister of Education in the Taleban Government. He was Mullah Muttaqui, about 36 years old, well educated, very articulate and fluent in Urdu. He advised that instead of one college, if this sum is spread over 15 institutions about 20,000 students will benefit. In case of Habibia College only 5000 students will be helped, ultimately; when it gets into full swing. We agreed to his proposal and he took us on a daylong tour of various destroyed facilities in and around Kabul.

Our first stop was Itiqlal College, built by the French at about the same time, but on a much grander scale. However, it was completely gutted and barely functional. Next stop was Madrassah Alia, which used to have more than 5000 students at one time. It was destroyed too, and a few hundred hardy students were on its rolls at present. We then visited a professional college on the outskirts of Kabul in similar condition. We asked Mullah Muttaqui to give us an estimate for restoration of these institutions and he said that a sum of 29 lakh Rupees will be required for the job if done through the civil works department in his Ministry. Contractors' estimate was in crores. This project was in hand when COF attacked Afghanistan.

Another important institution, the polytechnic institute of Kabul was taken up on priority for restoration. An appeal was launched by UTN through the fortnightly magazine *Jihad e Kashmir* that was responded to by Some Norwegian Muslims. They got in touch with us and we invited them to come and see for themselves and ascertain the needs. They came and we had a lengthy meeting with them in Islamabad. The sum required for this polytechnic was 1 million dollars; however preliminary work could be started with 100,000 in the first phase. They pledged this sum and planning to undertake this work had started, when the Attack came and everything stopped in its tracks. This was a particularly difficult operation, because of its technical nature and various other facets. One large (and rich) Saudi welfare organization 'Al Wafa' had tried its hand to set this institution up and failed. There head honcho Mr. Abdul Aziz told us that it was not possible to rehabilitate the Polytechnic at present. We then contacted the principal and staff of Rawalpindi Institute for Technology and discussed this problem with them. Their response was very encouraging and enthusiastic. They not only agreed to work on the project with us but also undertook to train the staff of the institute in Kabul and Rawalpindi as the need maybe. A governing body comprising of members from UTN, Afghan ministry of education and Rawalpindi Institute of Technology was formed.

The member nominated by the Afghan Education Ministry was Engineer Yousuf. He was associated with the Kabul Polytechnic for the last 25 years. He was being paid from 400 to 1000 rupees per month as per availability of funds with the Government. He had not been paid for the last 3 months due to paucity of funds. Whatever funds were available were being spent on repair and rehabilitation of schools, colleges and universities. This was being done with the consent of the teaching staff. They undertook to persevere and go along with the proposal because they trusted their Government. Sultan asked Engr. Yousuf as to why does he not leave and find a better employment elsewhere. He was a qualified and experienced engineer and getting a suitable employment commensurate with his qualifications was easy. He replied that he is managing at present by cultivating veggies on a plot of land that he owned adjacent to his house. His 2 sons take these to the vegetable market to sell on a cart. He had long and fond memories about this institution and never contemplated leaving. He was waiting for some God fearing person to come along and restore the Polytechnic to its past glory. Circumstances always change, they are never stagnant. One has to be patient to succeed.

Minister of education told us that after defence, education gets the maximum share of the limited budget. There were 1,500,000 students studying in 4000 schools all over Afghanistan at that time. For the education of girls Taleban had allocated all centrally located mosques in the cities. We were surprised to see one large mosque in Kabul where classes were being held for more than 1000 girls between Zuhr (midday) and Aser (afternoon) prayers. The Taleban Government was making admirable efforts with its meagre resources to restore to some semblance of normalcy the education system from primary to the university, throughout the country.

Kabul Medical College was back on its feet and functioning after an extended off and on closure. However it was facing huge problems because of the crippling and criminal sanctions imposed by the U.N. Availability of surgical implements was next to nothing. It was very difficult to put the graduating doctors through house jobs because of lack of even basic facilities in the few hospitals still functioning. A solution to circumvent this problem that was put in place by them was to put the students through a one-year basic medicine course and then send them to rural areas to set up their own practice or work in emergency medicine in the cities. This programme was akin to barefoot doctors of Mse Tung in China. They did a tremendous job at a time of crisis in China providing healthcare countrywide; besides it provided useful employment to the youth as a consequence.

Despite these *barefoot* doctors, there was no denying that need for qualified doctors and nurses was acute and Sultan discussed this problem with the head of Holy Family Hospital in Rawalpindi, Dr. Nisar. He was very sympathetic and understanding and offered to provide house jobs to any Afghan doctor who wanted one at his hospital. However this offer could not be taken up for lack of funds to facilitate Afghan doctors to come and live here for such jobs. Former principal of Rawalpindi Medical College and renowned surgeon Professor Iqbal was also consulted and requested to send doctors to Afghanistan to perform operations there so that Afghan doctors can learn by participation in such procedures. He agreed to the proposal in principle; however modalities remained to be worked out with him. But time ran out. Ex Surgeon General of the Army Dr. Najam and Dr. Malik of Pakistan Institute of Medical Sciences (PIMS) were also approached and they agreed to go and set up medical camps in Afghanistan to train doctors there and treat patients on the spot. But this entailed an expenditure of at least 20 million rupees. The Afghan Minister of Health when contacted said that he had no funds available but appreciated our efforts and pledged to cooperate fully if anything came out it, i.e. funds became available.

Another problem area was paucity of pharmaceutical supplies throughout the country. We contacted some pharmaceutical manufacturers in Pakistan and offered to introduce and facilitate them in Afghanistan to set up manufacturing facilities there. This offer was not taken up by any of them although this was a very lucrative commercial opportunity open to anybody enterprising enough to venture in this field. Medicine available within the country was sub standard and third-rate supplies were being exported to Afghanistan by unscrupulous elements from Pakistan in collaboration with their kin in Afghanistan. Before the Russian invasion Hoest, a German multinational pharmaceutical company had a large manufacturing facility near Kabul where standard medicine was produced for the country. It was a skeleton of its past now running at hardly one tenth of its designed capacity. Many Afghans had lost their limbs over the years because of the constant wars. There were no standard artificial limbs available within the country and those being used caused more pain and hardship instead of lessening it. One grave problem was lack of anaesthesia for the patients to be operated on. The only solution was that the patient's relatives held on to his hands and feet while the doctor cut and sewed him up. Thanks to the sanctions imposed, even anaesthesia was not allowed in to the country. There was no blood testing laboratory functioning in the country, therefore blood, even when available, could not be provided to the patients. Most of them died for lack of blood. Some NGOs were active in this field but all their efforts were not enough. The problems were too gigantic and most NGOs had already given up on that score.

We found that the Afghan people consumed too much medicine by force of habit. The reason was that doctors there had no means at their disposal to conduct diagnostic tests. They thus prescribed all possible remedial medications as indicated by looking at the patient. Cancer was also on the rise because of use of chemical and DU weapons over the last 20 years, continuously. Prime Minister of Afghanistan Mullah Rabbani died of cancer in August 2001. UTN undertook to provide medical cover to all the staff of Afghan Embassy in Islamabad. They did not have the funds to do so. Likewise a few cancer patients from Afghanistan, recommended by the Afghan Ambassador, were provided treatment by UTN. They regained health and were grateful, before they left for their country.

Once visiting Kabul Central Hospital, we met senior doctors there and discussed their predicament with them. They told us that people coming to the hospital expect prescribed medications given to them free of cost, as had been the norm in the past, before sanctions were imposed. When they find out to their dismay that no medicine is available, they get agitated and voices get raised. This happens almost daily and the doctors empathized with the people, because they knew that they had no money to buy medicine from the market. Situation in small towns and villages was even worse and children suffered the most.

We never came across a child specialist doctor anywhere in the country. Desperation written on the face of a mother of a sick child in Afghanistan in those days cannot be described in words. She had no one to turn to except Allah and nowhere to go except the graveyard to bury a piece of her. We found very few homeopathic doctors in the country and none practicing traditional Islamic medicine (Hikmat), anywhere. Some gentlemen from Pakistan expressed an interest in relief work to address these problems, but we advised them to help rebuild facilities there on a permanent basis. This provides gainful employment for many and destroyed facilities get resurrected for generations to come. Relief work creates and supports dependency and despondency.

Sultan participated in the Day of Independence celebrations in 2001 held on 19 August every year. He was invited along with a 20-member delegation headed by Gen. Hamid, a retired general of the Pakistan Army. The crowning event of these celebrations was the Military Parade held in the vast Eid-Gah of Kabul. The protocol officer conducting the Pakistan delegation was Mr. A.G Afghani, fluent in both Urdu and English and very dignified. Gen. Hamid said to him that Afghanistan has never been subjugated to any foreign occupying power, so how did this day of independence come about? He replied that the British tried 3 times to occupy Kabul and failed. First attempt was made in 1846 with Sikhs also joining in the effort, second time it was 1901 that the Brits tried again as they controlled most of India at that time. The last and third time was 1919, when the British mounted their biggest effort with overwhelming forces. They were desperate to occupy and control Kabul this time. One Mullah Shore Bazaar (pre cursor of present day Taleban) organized a sustained and determined resistance to oust the British forces. On 19 August 1919 the Afghans finally and decisively defeated the foreign invaders. For the Afghans it was an historic occasion, because they had defeated an empire on which the sun never set. Thus they decided to celebrate this as their day of deliverance (or independence) from all so-called super powers, present and future.

Discipline and organizing skill of the Taleban Authorities was evident on that day. There were very few traffic cops visible anywhere in the city or the parade grounds. But there was no chaos of any kind. People were in the hundreds of thousands and knew where to go to witness the parade. The then ministers for economics and administrative affaires Mullah Abdul Kabir Haqqani and Mullah Mohammad Hasan Akhund supervised the parade, respectively.

After recitation from the Holy Quran a message from Mullah Omar was read out in Pashto, in which he called upon the officials to do their duties diligently and serve the people. He asked the people to be patient, persevere in the face of hardship and promote Jihad at all levels, personal and national. After that national songs, without music, started blaring from speakers placed all over the grounds; but these appealed to cast and creed of the Pathans instead of projecting Islamic values. These were sung by popular poet singers such as Faqir Mohammad Darwesh and Bhagwan. This was disappointing and Sultan, ever so alert, told the Afghan Ulema attending the parade that the propagation of caste, creed and nationhood at the expense of Islam must be avoided. All such divisions within Islam are possible for recognition only, but these should never supersede Islamic international brotherhood that it stands for. The appeal towards cast and creed at the expense of Islam and superseding it will defeat the Taleban movement. This was a tactic employed by the enemies of Islam to defeat it from within; when they realized that it was not possible to do so from without. He raised this question with the Industries minister Mullah Saeed Ur Rehman Haqqani, author of many books and an accomplished scholar. He agreed and promised to correct the mistake by raising this issue of (Pathan) nationhood at an appropriate level and forum.

After this the parade started in earnest and first in was a column marching in old historical outfits displaying weapons of a bygone era, such as swords, bows and arrows, javelins etc. They were followed by regimented troops and even a naval contingent. Afghanistan is a land locked country, thus seeing a naval presence was intriguing. We were told that they man naval riverboat units on Amu Darya (river) on the border with Uzbekistan. Gen Hamid remarked that Taleban forces were fragmented in the past, now they seemed to be getting regimented which was a good sign. Last in were Air Force jets and they swooped really low, so low that the smoke from their after burners lingered on the parade ground for quite some time. It testified to their skill, daring and confidence in flying these old Russian built jets.

This military parade was an important milestone for the Taleban regime. On display were Russian built tanks, missiles and aircraft, which were left behind by them when they left the country. They had repaired most indigenously, which was a feat under the circumstances. We noticed that they made some additions and alterations to these weapons to operate in the local conditions. They had started local production on a limited scale as well. Regimentation is alien to Afghan culture; but we saw regiments with their own distinct identities for the first time in this parade. Afghans have been divided into different tribes, ethnic groups and lineages for centuries. Such ties take precedence over everything else. Each entity tends to fiercely defend its own territory, sometimes in tandem, sometimes not when faced with a common enemy. If these free spirits get united in regiments they will become more focused and a formidable force to contend with. They were getting more and more organized with time and experience and we felt that this organizing is going to help them in the days ahead.

In the first week of September, 2001 Sultan met the minister for economics, Mullah Abdul Kabir, in Jalalabad. He had plans with him to take out a large canal from Kuner to fall into Kabul, thus connecting both rivers and creating sufficient head for generation of 50 Megawatts of electricity for the region. An industrial park was also planned between Jalalabad and Torkhum and power for it was to be brought out from this 50 MW turbine. 20,000 acres of land would have become cultivable in this project, which was laying waste now. The estimated cost of this project was 80 million dollars. The funds were projected to be raised by liquidating Government Lands in and around Jalalabad. Survey had been completed and plans had been vetted. They wanted UTN to undertake and manage the actual construction.

A few months before this discussion an Afghan American citizen became the go-between for the Taleban and 2 US investors in an oil refinery project. The proposal on the anvil was for a 3000-barrel/ day refinery to be set up using old machinery and used equipment, at a cost of 15 million dollars. The actual cost for such a set-up was less than 3 million dollars. Mullah Saeed Ur Rehman Haqqani called us from Kabul for advice before signing the contract. He was told not to sign as a brand new refinery can be installed in half the cost projected. He was taken aback and requested the pleasure of our company in Kabul as soon as possible. On reaching Kabul Sultan apprised the minister and his staff about the scam he was about to get into. They were delighted to find out the truth and awarded this project to UTN too. A team of experts was put together and went to Afghanistan to redraw the project and come up with a realistic cost estimate. After a thorough study it was proposed to set up a brand new refinery with a capacity of 5000-barrel/ day at a cost of 8 million dollars. If scrap from Afghanistan could be collected and used another 4 million dollars could be saved. All fabrication work was projected to be undertaken in Pakistan and Afghanistan costing in

Rupees. Foreign exchange required was about 1 million dollars only. This was an eye opener for the Taleban authorities, and the joy and excitement it created in them was gratifying. 12 Afghan and 2 Pakistani engineers were earmarked for this project and they started working in a week's time. The Government proudly announced on the Radio *Sada e Shariah* that Afghanistan was now in a position to fabricate and install an oil refinery, indigenously, in collaboration with UTN.

After the death of the Prime Minister, Mullah Rabbani in August 2001 two deputy prime ministers were appointed. One was the minister for economics Maulvi Abdul Kabir and the other was for administration Maulvi Mohammad Hasan Akhund. Maulvi Abdul Kabir was the Governor for the provinces of Logar, Jalalabad and Nauman also. He was reputed to be a go-getter and very energetic. As discussed elsewhere, he met Sultan and requested him to help in building a hydro power project near Jalalabad for generation of 50 MW of electricity to supply power to an industrial park planned on the road to Torkhum. This plan was drawn up in 1976 but could not be implemented because of self-serving corrupt governments, which followed one another since. The project was feasible and UTN undertook to complete it in record time. He also had another project in mind on Bamiyan River and took Sultan and 2 of his colleagues, Shoaib and Iqbal (both civil engineers) to have a look at it. After an arduous journey from Kabul they reached the dam site. However data available with the officials was sketchy and many details, like seasonal flow pattern of the river, height of the dam required generating at least 10 MW etc., remained to be worked out. For this a hydro station was required to be built at the site to collect and collate data for a feasibility report. Sultan asked Maulvi Abdul Kabir to make one at a place he earmarked for him. He issued immediate orders for it to be constructed and delegated responsibility there and then, telling Sultan to provide the blueprint so that work could start earnestly. Sultan was impressed by the speed of these decisions and the readiness of all assembled there to assume responsibility.

This was a remote but green area because of the river and regular rainfall. There were about 70 people gathered there for the survey; some were officials and others were the locals of the area who had lived there all their lives and knew the place intimately. Precisely the kind of people required answering searching questions asked by the visitors from Pakistan for construction of the dam. It was an amazing ability of the Taleban authorities that they were always able to get across to the right kind of people on such occasions. People came forth without fear or favour and there used to be no inhibitions of any kind. Discussions were forthright and open but respectful. Lunch was served and everybody joined in drivers, peons, ministers and ordinary people; it was difficult to tell who was who. The local notables demanded a rural hospital for the area as there was none nearby and the sick had to be carried long distances. Maulvi Abdul Kabir asked UTN for help, as he had no funds available immediately for the job. Sultan promised that he will look into it when he gets back to Pakistan. On return he talked to two friends of his in USA and they pledged enough funds for a hospital, a doctor and a nurse. Plans were drawn up and ready to go when foreign forces invaded Afghanistan. Rest is history.

Deputy Governor of Jalalabad Hafiz Mohammad came with a request to buy road-building machinery, as he was building the road from Jalalabad to Kabul. He was asked to come to Islamabad to have a look at the machinery for himself. He came and we asked him what is it exactly, that was required. He indicated that he required a road roller, a leveller and a mixing machine immediately. We told him it would cost a packet; did he have the money? He said that he had more than enough and told us as to how he was able to raise that kind of money. He brought most businessmen of Kabul and Jalalabad together and told them that this road can be built in a year if they come up with the money now, otherwise it will take another 3 years at least. They offered to pay the toll tax in advance for the road to raise cash. Hafiz Mohammad told them that they should start paying this tax voluntarily for every type of vehicle now plying on the road themselves. They agreed and every month 8,000,000 Rupee were being deposited with him for the last 3 months. The only condition they imposed was that this money should be used for the road only, to which he agreed. This indicates the degree of trust reposed by the people in the Taleban Government. We located all 3 of these machines for him in Lahore, in almost mint condition at a good price. He liked them and called the PM from Lahore for his approval. He approved on phone; Hafiz Mohammad paid cash on the spot and left for Jalalabad. We made arrangements for delivery in about 5 day's time. But then circumstances changed drastically and we do not know if the delivery was made or not, to this day.

SETTING UP THE MILL

Work on the flourmill started in earnest in November 2000 in Kandahar Industrial Zone on Airport Road outside the city. There was no water or electric connection and no asphalt road access to the site. We had to start with boring for ground water with 2 generators brought in from Pakistan. Workers lived in tents and encountered snakes, scorpions and poisonous spiders at night. One spider was especially dangerous; it travelled over any exposed skin infecting it from the inside with no sign on the outside. This caused intense pain, fever and swelling rendering the victim incapacitated and unable to work. Wild dogs, jackals and foxes roamed the area by nightfall. We got used to their shrieks after some time and slept through it all. There were low mountain ranges at our backyard and in January 2001 snow came down changing the whole scenery but bringing in biting cold.

Very little by way of fittings for the mill, was available in the city. Even screws had to be brought in from Pakistan along with all the heavy machines. Transportation was by way of trucks and these were allowed to travel all the way from anywhere in Pakistan to Kandahar, without off loading or cross loading. This became possible after we were able to obtain permission from authorities in Kandahar to allow our trucks to travel all the way to Kandahar from Pakistan. It was a great relief and one headache lessened. On the Pakistan side our cargo was thoroughly checked and scrutinized before allowing it to proceed across the border, in the beginning. Once across the border going was smooth, except for the bumpy roads. After a while we were delighted to find that while checking our cargo the staff on the Pakistan side became very helpful when they found out that it was for a flourmill in Kandahar, which we were setting up. They would refuse any graft or even (the usual) tips and said that it was for a worthy cause, so you can go. There were no import duties or any other levies imposed by the Afghanistan Government throughout the installation, as promised. We however took a list of all our cargo to the municipal offices once in a while for record and registration, with a copy to the provincial D.G Mines and Industries.

This D.G Mines and Industries was a very remarkable and genial man. His office in the city was always full of people drinking tea. He sorted out disputes there and then quite openly, in front of everybody. He kept no security guards or peons/ doormen for his office, but always carried an officially issued Kalashnikov with him, out of habit. He told us that he has carried a gun with him always from age 18 onwards. He was now more than 50 years old. He came to demarcate the land for us himself and told us to plant trees, as he was allocating us a green belt to do so. When we asked him to make access roads for ease of communication, he said I can give you land you make the roads yourself. He was a veteran of the Russian campaign as well and was deadly against any more fighting in Afghanistan or elsewhere in the world.

Civil works were completed by about March 2001 and erection of machinery started there after. A 20 KV line passed nearby but there was no transformer available for supplying power to the mill, with the local electric supply utility. This too was manufactured in Pakistan and trucked very carefully to be installed by Pakistani technicians and local labour. With the passage of time security personnel manning check posts became familiar with our truckloads carrying all that machinery for the mill. Trucking thus became easier and less time consuming up to the flourmill. However the truckers we hired from Lahore and Punjab were the most devious and tried to pull a fast one if they could. Balochi transport (trucking) companies were found to be quite honest by Punjabi standards. We used to look for these Balochi truckers with experience and hindsight. Shipping from Karachi was also not much of a problem, as truckers there were either from Baluchistan or Sarhad (NWFP).

During the course of erection of the flourmill, an agreement was required to be signed between us and the Authorities laying down terms and conditions for running of the mill. This was to be signed by the Minister for food and agriculture on behalf of the Government. We decided to go see him at his residence in the city. On arrival we found a mud brick house with no doors on the outside, just old soiled curtains fluttering in the wind. We were ushered in a sitting room with bare walls and a cotton carpet to sit on and served with fruit. A lone worn out pedestal fan was whining and running in a corner providing some relief from heat. A younger brother of the Minister was serving us with fruit and green tea. We saw the simplicity of it all, and estimated that the living standards of Ministers were the same as the general populace of the Country. That was probably the primary reason this regime was so popular; the people were able to identify with them.

Another reason for their popularity was the easy approachability and openness of the officials at every level. We found them to be free of any pretences or notions of their infallibility. They were making mistakes and knew it; but were learning fast. Given time they would steady them and improve, we thought. However, time was not on their side, as indeed it was not on ours. We also met the Minister's 3 sons aged 5 to 10, who were playing outside as we arrived; they had no shoes on and wearing just long coarse cloth (*Khaddar*) shirts. The Minister arrived after about 20 minutes, from a meeting with Mullah Omer, and sat down with us to chat. He agreed to all of our submissions and decided to sign the Agreement the next day at a time and place of our choosing. Indeed, the next day he came with one of his Assistants at the appointed hour promptly, and signed the agreement first before offering it to us to sign. Both of them, the Minister and his

Assistant, came in an unmarked old Toyota car without any security detail. There were just two of them and the Minister was driving himself. They left as they came, after staying with us for about half an hour.

There was no hotel or motel worth staying in the city of Kandahar. Staying in tents in the wild, where the Industrial Park was located, was not easy. Fortunately, the Consul General of Pakistan turned out to be a Godsend. He was very knowledgeable about Afghan affaires and had been posted in Kabul and Mazar-e-Sharif before coming to Kandahar. He knew the Taleban regime intimately, their weaknesses and strong points. He almost ordered me to move in with him in his large house, till such time that proper accommodation is laid out in the mill and becomes liveable. He knew my younger brother who retired as an Ambassador in the Foreign Service of Pakistan. Over time as we discussed the situation in the Country at length, I gained valuable insights about what was going on both inside and outside the Government. I also met our Consul posted in Herat, known simply as Col. Imam (not his real name). He was a veteran of the Soviet era and had helped conduct that war, endearing himself to the Afghan Mujahedeen in the process. Sometimes Intelligence Agencies' officials also participated in these discussions.

One refrain I heard over and over again was that no foreign power, however resourceful could force its will on Afghan people. Invaders can win battles in this Country but they will always lose the war. History, Geography, Culture and Tradition were the reasons quoted. These were the same reasons, which were holding this regime together in spite of so much pressure from within and without, they said. There were more volunteers than weapons (to arm them) to fight the Northern Alliance. Taleban had no funds left to sustain the campaign any longer and push out Ahmad Shah Masood the de facto Northern Alliance leader, once and for all. Two Arabs posing as journalists in Badakhshan province finally killed him. But it was too late by then, as US attacked Afghanistan 2 days after his death.

The role of the Ministry to curb evil and promote virtues was generally felt as a misguided and ill-informed attempt at coercing the people to adhere to Islamic values. In our discussions with the people high and low, it was quite apparent that it was impossible to force Islamic values down the throats of people when they were not ready to accept them. Practices like forcing people to ritual prayers (5 times a day) and keeping of beards by all men were not popular, and resented by the populace. Culture and tradition was stronger and more deeply rooted than Islamic religious values. If these values coincided with tradition so much the better, if not, religion (Islam) took a back seat. Attempts at rectifying this attitude by the Ministry were not popular and were backfiring. I saw shopkeepers shutting themselves in their shops, at the time of prayers, to avoid confronting religious police, who forced them to join prayers at the nearby mosque. Some of these shop owners, who had lived in Pakistan for some time, praised the set up there; where nobody forced anybody to follow these and other common Islamic practices. They wanted to send all personnel belonging to this Ministry to Pakistan for training. However, generally speaking the religious police adopted a lenient view and they would let go, after only a warning to most of those caught.

Come September, and the mill was almost ready to start production. However, because of our peculiar situation it was delayed for a whole month. Bits and pieces required for finishing touches had to be brought in from Pakistan causing delays. Things were becoming more and more unpredictable as events unfolded after 9/11, in the end an attack by US forces became inevitable in October. I was in Quetta at that time and saw the preparations for it, from the vantage point of Serena hotel there. I was staying at a place across the road from the hotel and frequently visited there for meals and various other chores. The most expensive rooms were taken over by the US military and media groups. They installed all their gadgetry in and around the hotel to transmit live coverage of the operation back to USA and rest of the world. There was an atmosphere of a great show (like a Circus) being staged in the coming days. Predictions floating around were that it should be over in a couple of weeks at most. That was October 2001 and it is not over yet, a lapse of almost ten years. All those expert opinions I heard in there back then, came to a naught in the end.

The mill was in trial production when the aerial attacks started in October 2001. I had to travel between Kandahar and Quetta frequently because there were a thousand things to attend to and in a hurry. Conflicting news were floating around as to the exact date of the attack. I found a remarkable amount of calm and a lack of panic amongst the general population in Afghanistan. People were not overly worried, as they knew that it was going to be an aerial campaign for the most part. In the official circles, it was business as usual, leaving all to fate as it were? The people I talked to in Kandahar all said that they had nowhere else to go. A common refrain was that we were born here and we shall die here. To the question of avoiding the attack by succumbing to all the demands put forward by UN and US authorities, almost everybody said "no". The underlying theme was that if all of Afghanistan including the Government, stood on its head the attack will still take place. The mood was that when rape is inevitable, better sit back and enjoy it. There was a lot of sympathy and understanding for this point of view of Afghans in Pakistan. I saw young men crossing over to Afghanistan in hordes to join the Afghans in their hour of need. All border crossing points were open and there was no checking of any kind, which was a blessing as mostly women and children were entering Pakistan for shelter, while young men were going to the other side.

We continued with trials even after the attack started and I went in to see the results from Quetta, travelling by road as usual. There was no dearth of taxis for Kandahar to take me there. I did not see any Taleban forces on the road, a distance of 101 kilometres from the border up to the mill. Trials were successful but the quality of wheat was not up to the mark and had to be replaced. Contract negotiations were started but our suppliers all left for their hometowns when the attack came. They were mostly from the North of the Country and that is where they went; places like Herat, Torghundi, Mazar e Sharif etc. It was speculated that these places were relatively safer than Kabul and Kandahar and areas adjacent to them. Which turned out to be true, but we never saw those men after that.

In March of 2001 a new basic hotel opened in Kandahar, near chowk Shahidan. It was named Hotel Noor Jehan, after wife of a Moghul Emperor Jahangir of India, who gained fame because of dispensing justice to the high and low even-handedly. I became their regular customer and got to know them to the extent that they sometimes gave me the keys of the entire hotel, when they were going visiting their relations, who lived nearby. The rooms had 2 beds and 2 chairs only and no table of any kind. There was running water in the toilet, but the water drained onto the floor before running out through the drain hole in a corner. There was no ceiling fan, a pedestal fan was provided however, which was a great relief. In winters it became biting cold and a single rod electric heater was provided, which was plugged in when there was power available. The staff managed without a fan in summers or a heater in winters, which testified to their hardiness and forbearance. This trait of forbearance could be observed everyday in the common folks of Kandahar. For example, even beggars on the streets displayed this spirit everyday. They were clearly in need and most were disabled, but they would not approach you with outstretched hands (as is the practice in

Pakistan), for a handout. One could see a man sitting at a respectable distance from the road on a blanket spread out in front of him, his head bowed as if in shame and keeping mum all the time. Anybody who wanted to give alms approached him, not vice versa.

THE ATTACK

Afghanistan's population stood at 20 million at the time of Soviet invasion. At the end of 10 years when they left, they had killed 2 million people and 5 million were injured. There were 5 million women and children who were widowed/ orphaned during this brutal invasion[4]. They had nowhere to go and no means of livelihood. 6 million able bodied men were unemployed in 2001. With this background mighty USA decided to have a go at these hapless people. The attack by US forces started after sunset on 07 October 2001. They were attacking by standoff weapons at night only, to begin with. The reason was that ground intelligence was not available or sketchy at best. They used high tech weapons, but accuracy was not very good. After a few days they gained confidence and started attacking by day. However, The Taleban had amassed junk Russian era tanks and other similar paraphernalia for them to bomb. Working tanks and other vehicles were spread out very thinly in and around Kandahar; however, these were not very many as most of the working military hardware was busy on the Northern front.

The Northern Alliance was strengthened and joined by the CIA Forces to drive back Taleban forces from the front. Of course they were routed quickly and fell back helter skelter. Many foot soldiers were captured and stuffed like sardines in steel containers, where they died of suffocation. Vast graves were then dug in the sands of the vast desert *Dasht e Leili* near Shiberghan and Mazar e Sharif and this dead cargo was emptied into them by dump trucks. Those murdered so mercilessly were mostly volunteers from Pakistan, Central Asia and the Middle East besides Afghanistan. CIA was very active in all these operations, and some of its agents were also killed in the melee.

---

[4] Wikipedia, *Soviet War in Afghanistan.*

Everyone was left on his own to save his skin as best as he could. Very few managed to save themselves and survived. Some of the survivors and eyewitnesses were later interviewed and reports were filed by magazines like Newsweek[5], ICRC and various human rights organizations. The occupying forces for obvious reasons allowed no serious investigation.

One large group took refuge in underground shelters in Mazar e Sharif to avoid being killed. It was November and very cold. Abdul Rashid Dostum, the local warlord got a chance to get even with Taleban for ousting him from power. He ordered cold water released from fire hoses into the shelters. Those who came out were shot at sight and thrown back in. These were the lucky ones; they drowned dead, as against those inside who died of cold or drowning. No prisoners were taken as a matter of policy. Some of the Taleban fighters shot each other to avoid being tortured and killed. There are some witnesses still living that went through all this barbarity but they cannot speak. Maybe they will be able to tell their story in the future, when foreign forces leave, circumstances change and they are allowed to talk.
 Most of those killed did not carry any weapons, some had dropped them, others had lost them and all were volunteers fighting for a cause, right or wrong: I do not know. All these so called Taleban fighters, though highly motivated, had scant or no military training at all. But motivation alone did not prove to be enough. A report, dated 07 May 2002 written by Mr. Niko Price of Associated Press is quite revealing and available on the internet[6].

---

[5] *Newsweek* 26 August, 2002, by John Barry and Babak Dehghanpisheh.

[6] UN team finds evidence of summary execution, suffocation in mass graves by Niko Price of AP. RAWA news at http://www.rawa.org

A delegation made up of doctors and nurses from Pakistan was put together by Pakistan Islamic Medical Association (PIMA) on 8th of October 2001 to provide relief to the injured. They set up camps along the border with Afghanistan in the hope that the injured will be brought to them for treatment. They discovered, to their horror, that Pakistani Authorities had sealed the border and were not allowing the injured or dying to crossover for treatment. PIMA is a member of Federation of Islamic Medical Associations (FIMA), which comprised of such associations belonging to 26 countries, at that time. Medical Associations from Jordan, Saudi Arabia, Malaysia and Indonesia pledged all kind of help in men and material to PIMA for relief work. A Malaysian medical team under the banner of MERCY took the lead and came to Pakistan on a fact-finding tour. They were shown the camps set up by PIMA inside Pakistan, along the border, but without patients. After further consultations it was decided to set up treatment centres inside Afghanistan manned by Pakistani staff and funded by FIMA. This team managed to cross into Afghanistan on 31st October 2001, after facing lot of difficulties at the hands of various Pakistani Agencies who were instructed to prevent any humanitarian help reaching Afghanistan.

They heaved a sigh of relief on reaching Afghanistan and were handed over a dispensary to manage and run, near the border on the Afghanistan side. This they did and raced towards Kabul to set up and start the treatment centres there, as time was running out. To their surprise they found all markets and commercial centres open, with throngs of people going about their business in all cities and towns along the way up to Kabul. On reaching Kabul they first went out to see Dr. Khalid, a dentist from U.S.A, who had come down from there to help manage and run medical facilities in and around Kabul. He was the head of an organization Global Medical Association, which was funding his trip and providing medical supplies. He took them to see the ultra modern set up of Aljazeera Television, on the premises of Kabul Intercontinental hotel, which was impressive.

According to Dr. Khalid there were 6 working hospitals in Kabul at that time. The 400 bed Military Hospital was fully functional, another Wazir Akbar Khan Hospital was barely managing and a third hospital was being run by ICRC. The rest 3 hospitals were in a very bad state: out of these one was handed over to a team from Qatar to rehabilitate and run, one was with him and he was busy restoring it to make it functional. That left out one hospital for the PIMA team to improve, manage and run, if they could. It was the 70 beds Ibn-e Sina Chest hospital, in a dilapidated state. The PIMA team decided to transform it into a Trauma Centre as there was none in Kabul at that time. Its location was also ideal for an emergency centre, as it was surrounded by hills on three sides, not an easy target for an attack from the air. With this in mind the team members went to see the Taleban Minister for Health Maulvi Syed Asmatullah Asim. He approved all their plans and they undertook to pay one-year advance salaries to all the staff of the hospital.

They planned to make this a model hospital for Afghanistan with all the latest equipment, specialist doctors from Pakistan and most important of all a clean and disinfected environment to work in. Dr. Khalid, the dentist from U.S.A offered to provide all ambulances needed and to pay for all civil works required to make this hospital look like a hospital. His offer was gratefully accepted. Lastly this PIMA team met a senior doctor in charge of epidemic control and contagious diseases. They asked him about women's education so that some of them could later qualify as doctors to work in Afghanistan. He told them that Taleban wanted to set up adequate and enough facilities for women's education, but they do not have the funds. We all would like to have our womenfolk treated by Afghan women doctors, and no Talib was against that notion. It was a dream under the prevailing conditions, when the salary of the most senior doctor in Afghanistan was Rs. 12,000/- only, because of lack of funds.

The fact finding trip by this PIMA team was a success, but it all came to a naught in the end, because the Taleban left Kabul the same day and it fell to the invading foreign forces. On their return trip they stayed in Jalalabad for one night and were told that all Taleban were leaving for the mountains to wage a long and protracted war against the invaders. The taxi driver they travelled with showed them a lone grave of a dear friend of his who died fighting the Russian invaders. He was a taxi driver too like himself and he said that if the Americans land in Afghanistan he will give up his taxi and join in the holy war against the enemy.

The aerial attack was mostly limited to Kandahar, Kabul and the adjoining areas. Pretty quickly suitable targets to attack were exhausted. There were not many targets to begin with, and I saw funny things happening because of it. The fighter pilots attacking with these very sophisticated and expensive weapons would sometimes discharge them on plain ground and/ or use them against insignificant targets. For example there was a single pole antenna on top of a hill behind our mill. It was hit by a million dollar missile from the air. The antenna was not worth more than a couple of thousand dollars. The resulting explosion caused some glass panes to be broken in the factories in the area. Very expensive munitions were routinely used to destroy mud-thatched houses which were empty at times. I managed to take some pictures during the day when bombing stopped. One civilian oil tanker truck carrying diesel fuel for civilian use was burnt to a cinder after being hit by a precision guided missile on Kandahar- Herat road. Another trailer truck carrying veggies and condiments to the main vegetable market was targeted by these weapons and torn to pieces, including the driver and his aid. I saw it soon after the incident and the scene presented a surreal appearance: turmeric powder, chilli powder and veggies mixed with human blood spread all over the tarmac. They had removed the bodies tracing lines of dripping blood pointing towards the direction of removal. Then I saw a mud house nearby with holes to dry grapes hung by strings inside to make *kishmish* (dried grapes) destroyed for no apparent reason. "What a waste of resources" I remember thinking. The ammo being used to bomb the cities and being discharged sometimes to lighten the plane for the return journey near the city of Kandahar, in uninhabited areas on plain ground, were mostly made up of depleted Uranium (DU ammunition[7]). They had markings on them which warned of hazards of nuclear material, with instructions for its handling.

Our Flourmill was the highest building in the area and it was left untouched like so many other industrial structures belonging to concerns large and small, far and near. Later in the attack helicopters were introduced and they used the flourmill building as a visual beacon to fix their position, on way to their destinations. We got used to counting their numbers and telling their types as they flew over. A movie was shown some time after the attack about Special Forces conducting a secret operation in Kandahar area. It was ostensibly to show how the US Forces were trying to apprehend Mullah Omer and his close associates. I later got a chance to see the place where this operation was conducted and shown to the world by almost every TV channel worth mentioning. I was stunned to find out that it was actually a total failure with terrible consequences. The house selected was wrong, the place visited was wrong, the whole thing was a public relations exercise gone horribly wrong. Or maybe it was staged to boost the ebbing

---

[7] Heather Wokusch, *America's shameful legacy of radioactive weaponry.* June 13, 2010. www.heatherwokusch.com; & *Depleted Uranium Ammunition in Afghan War: New Evidence.* 21 July, 2009. www.globalresearch.ca

morale of the attacking forces. Absolutely unconcerned and innocent civilians were butchered in their sleep, including women and children.

It was evident that nothing of consequence was achieved in the attack by night using infra red as no Taleban leader was apprehended or found. Large sums of money were paid to some people acting as informers for the attackers. This did not work out because these people pocketed the money and informed the Taleban leadership before informing their paymasters. This way they provided accurate information as to their location except for one slight oversight: they kept their former bosses informed about what information they were providing. Revenge also played a part in this information providing game. When one party wanted to wreck vengeance on another, for whatever reason, it gave the co-ordinates to the Americans to attack them, labelling them as Taleban or their sympathizers.

Some errand boys such as drivers, dispatch riders or the like working for thrills and a living for Al Qaeda were apprehended and handed over to US authorities for torture etc. One such driver of Osama Bin Laden was tried and sentenced to a long prison term by a court in the US after being held at Guantanamo for 7 years without trial. These were ordinary people who had been misguided but were actually looking for adventure[8]; they have now been turned into heroes for a large part of the world. They were not terrorists by any stretch of imagination. One can call them radical revolutionaries, maybe, but not terrorists. 'Terrorism' as a euphemism is now the monopoly of all politicians; they use it to *terrorize* their own populations to achieve political

---

[8] Wright, Lawrence, "They included as well the curious, the holiday fighters, the students looking for an exciting way to spend their break." *The Looming Tower,* 109. Penguin Books,2007.

mileage. It is more than obvious that injustice is the root cause of all this radicalization. Remove the injustice and all violence will cease. On several occasions our bill was quietly paid by these same people (Arabs) living in Kabul and Kandahar in restaurants where we went in for lunch or dinner. They would simply pay the fare to the proprietor and leave without introducing themselves. On finding out, we would tell the manager in charge of these eateries to return the money paid, but he invariably said that it was not possible for him as he did not know the antecedents of those who have paid and left.

The most plausible explanation of 9/11 I have come across is that it was planned and executed by 15 Arabs and 4 others. All of them are gone now, so we will never find out the real truth. These young men saw the atrocities being committed on a daily basis by Israeli Jews with full US backing on helpless Palestinians and elsewhere and decided to do something about it. The hatred felt by them was so intense that they decided to give their life away to lessen its intensity. They did not seek any help and/ or had nothing to do with the secretive entity (Al Qaeda) to execute the spectacular fireworks of 9/11. Providently they were in a position to carry out the daring plan, although not a very ingenious one, with a fair amount of efficiency. All that talk about linkages between Al Qaeda on one hand and Afghanistan, Iraq and elements in Pakistan on the other, is akin to looking for "Weapons of Mass Destruction" in Iraq. No Government or Organization or Al Qaeda was involved, that is why it was so difficult to foretell or foresee its coming. These men (probably) sat down in a Dubai café and in Munich in Germany and planned the whole thing. That is why attempts to establish linkages and collect (forensic) evidence against those now incarcerated have all failed.

The accuracy of the precision-guided weapons was not so precise from the start. But it suffered as the war wore on.

Some buildings hit inside the city were fit for demolition anyway; people living in the adjoining streets jokingly thanked the US warplanes for such an expansive and expensive demolition. These buildings had no economic or strategic value for such attacks. Some isolated and already damaged uninhabited shacks outside Kandahar airport were bombed to extinction, and it was reported that the communications network of Taleban regime has been destroyed by US pilots in their state of the art flying machines. People had a hearty laugh at this news, and it became a popular joke to tell in a gathering. People slowly got used to these shows and the subsequent news flashes and started losing interest in the war as it wore on. They were resigned to their fate from the beginning, and now a degree of satisfaction set in, that they had made the right choice, i.e. to stay. There was news of a ground assault by US forces, which never materialized in 2001. The Taleban leadership decided to go into hiding in plain sight after they saw the inevitable outcome, which was coming their way. A gap of a few days was created when they left and the new set up was not yet in place. Fear of a return of the warlords gripped most of the southern parts of the Country. This fear dissipated quickly however, when the deposed Taleban established an effective administrative control in all the rural and remote areas and started dispensing justice. Remember that 50% of Afghanistan is rural and 30% is remote.

The reason that the Industrial area was not bombed and the airport only sparingly was that the occupying forces planned to use these areas to their advantage later. They took over the airport and immediately started work on establishment of a large air base there. All supplies to build it came from Pakistan or through it in large and heavy trailer trucks. However the road from Quetta to Kandahar was not up to the mark for such an activity. The portion from Quetta to the Pak/ Afghan border was partially hilly as well. This road up to the border was strengthened and re built with funds provided by the US authorities. An Indian company built the portion from the border up to Kandahar. All the labour, semi skilled and some skilled manpower for these jobs came from Pakistan. Some of these men working on the airport project lived on our mill premises, and they provided a fairly good idea of what was going on inside. There were Afghan labourers too, working inside the airport area. It was very easy for the Taleban regime to fade into the background and mix with the crowd.

From October 2001 onwards about 200 Taleban fighters are being killed every week on average as reported in the press. That means 200 into 54 into 9, i.e. 97,200 have been killed so far in 9 years. This is a significant number to contend with, but ground reality is something else. Out of this grand total of 97,200, 75% were unconnected civilians including women and children. That means 72,900 innocents have been killed so far[9]. Such practices create more enemies than friends for the occupation forces and provide a fertile ground for recruitment of more fighters for the Taleban. It is now an established fact that there is no dearth of fighters who are willing to lay down their lives to get rid of the occupation forces in Afghanistan. There is a local saying, which says that a man who is naked is not afraid of the river (that his clothes will get wet). The kind of governance system that US authorities want to bring to Afghanistan is alien to their culture. The only workable and fair (governance) system provided in recent past, was by the Taleban regime.

It is an established fact that the ex- Taleban regime in Afghanistan had had nothing to do with 9/11 attacks at any stage of the operation. Some Arabs, including Osama Bin Laden, helped them (the Taleban) and came to their rescue out of compassion and their adherence to Islamic values.

---

[9] Dr. Gideon Polya, www.Countercurrents.org, 07 October, 2007

Pakistani Intelligence agencies also helped out as a matter of policy, thus creating enduring ties that have withstood the test of time so far. It has turned out to be an investment for the future and is likely to pay hefty dividends once the scenario changes. I myself found these people (Afghan Taleban) to be very reasonable, honest and patient in their day-to-day dealings. Their approach to life's problems was so down to earth that it surprised us at times. When I expressed my concerns about the safety of huge investments that we were bringing to Afghanistan in one of our several meetings with various Ministers of the regime; the reply I got was amazing to say the least. Since I have had experience of dealing with the authorities in Pakistan in similar situations it was heartening and encouraged us to engage in other projects in the Country in earnest. Imagine a tax free, corruption free, safe and secure environment to do business in.

What this regime had achieved was in many ways similar to an atmosphere of incorruptible poverty that prevailed during the reign of the 2nd Caliph Omar bin Khattab[10] (May Allah be pleased with him). Reports in the press about capital punishments for petty crimes and cutting off of hands for theft etc are simply not true. Although we saw some such punishments being carried out, but those were reserved for habitual and repeat offenders (psychopaths) and only when their crime was proven beyond any shadow of doubt. The courts strictly adhered to due process of the law. The courts were quite independent and respected by ordinary citizens. Only a couple of capital punishments were carried out in six years, but then this eradicated all major crime completely and brought about a crime free environment.

---

[10] Barnaby Rogerson. *The Heirs of the Prophet (pbuh), 2.* Little, Brown UK Ltd., 2nd impression.

There were some hardliners in the Taleban regime, but they were few and far outnumbered by the moderates. We found these moderates to be pragmatic and practical, but they had a difficult time arguing with the hardliners, because of prevailing circumstances. The hardliners were of the view that no amount of leniency or accommodation by them will work out in the end. Any concessions made by them will be viewed as a sign of weakness. They admitted that they cannot win militarily, but argued that then the occupation forces also cannot stay forever. Sacrifices will be required, but if history is any guide, that is a price Afghans know well how to pay. Battle for the hearts and minds of the people of Afghanistan was lost, shortly after the war started, by the invading forces, because of the atrocities committed. Too much collateral damages and operations based on genocide were the cause. It is becoming increasingly possible that the expense of the war will break the back of the occupying forces, as predicted by the hardliners in 2001. The moderates however wanted to reach an understanding with the International Community at large to save the people from hardships of an unwanted war. War was indeed imposed on Afghanistan in the end, causing immense suffering and hardship for the people. A people who were too occupied in making both ends meet and had no time on their hands for politics or war. They just wanted to be left alone to survive on one dollar or less a day.

We found a remarkable amount of absence of animosity towards the West before the attack. People talked about the injustice of sanctions and the ensuing hardships, but they had taken them in their stride and were beginning to get used to them. Besides a lot of the sanctions imposed were cosmetic and effects of others were being negated by imports from Pakistan. Once Sultan asked the Afghan officials about the activities of Osama Bin Laden before the attack and they told him that he was busy these days in rehabilitation of widows and orphans. He had nothing to do anymore with weapons and fighting. Some members of our delegation expressed a desire to see him; but they were told that there was a prohibition on that and were disallowed. Even the hatred generated by the Russians against them, by their atrocious policies was waning. Most Afghans used to fall silent when questioned about the times and deeds of the Soviet Union. Their priority was to develop their country and bring it at par with others in the region.

It is regrettable and tragic that, it all fell apart after 9/11 occurred. To blame the Taleban for it or to establish linkages was foolhardy. But it was done for whatever reasons and the consequences are still with us. AL QAEDA or Taleban did not have the time and resources to plan and execute 9/11, when it occurred. To us, it is still a mystery that may never be solved in the true sense. After the attack it became obvious to us that weak and poor nations struggling to survive and make some headway have no place in the present day world set up. All their long and hard efforts over the years can be wiped out by powerful arrogant nations in days for whimsical reasons. Greed also plays a part in it. During the Russian occupation 2 to 3 million cubic feet of gas was being taken to USSR daily free of cost, from Afghanistan. We felt that USA will do the same if they could, and Sultan wrote a treatise on it in the October 16 issue of the Urdu fortnightly *Jihad e Kashmir*. The struggle against Russian occupation organized by Afghan Mujahedeen and CIA hijacked Al Qaeda while it was underway, because they rightly saw an opportunity here to get rid of the USSR as a rival once and for all. American contribution is limited to shortening the conflict only. It was otherwise waged, managed and controlled from within Afghanistan with Pakistan's help.

Two commanders of Northern Alliance Mohammad Afghan and Mohammad Hanif defected and joined the Taleban at the start of the hostilities. None went the other way, despite intense efforts in terms of free cash distribution (in US dollars) and promises of a rosy future in the USA. Professor Sayyaf practically joined the Alliance (NA) although he disliked US policy in Afghanistan, but Hikmatyar did not; his sympathies were with the Taleban. Generals Fahim and Dostum were left overs from the communist regimes as were most of the Northern Alliance Commanders. Professor Rabbani was helpless and rendered ineffective because of his past associations, although he too was against foreign intervention in Afghanistan.

Most of the foot soldiers with the Alliance did not like the lifestyle of their commanders and there were many incidents of insubordination, summary trials and hasty executions in the ranks. An intense effort was launched by the invading forces to alienate the general population from Taleban authorities, but it failed because of two reasons. One was that the people considered Taleban as one of their own and foreigners have always been looked at suspiciously in Afghanistan. The other reason was the peace and tranquillity (although with poverty, imposed from outside), which prevailed during the entire Taleban regime. A corruption free environment with quick dispensation of justice is what the people were nostalgic about. In this effort for the hearts and minds of the people cash and influence was freely used. Most of the time people just pocketed the money, but did not change their mindset. The people of Afghanistan, we found were singularly and famously single minded.

On 1st November 2001 a delegation of 23 journalists comprising of teams from BBC, CNN, AP, AFP, ABC, Reuters, NNI and a few others from Pakistan visited Kandahar to assess the situation first hand, on the invitation of the Taleban. A summary of the report filed by veteran journalist Mr. Tahir Khan of NNI, on his return from Kandahar is what follows:

They travelled to Quetta and entered from Chaman into Afghanistan via Spin Boldok. They were surprised to find that the large bazaar in Spin was partially open for business at midnight. On their way to Kandahar headlights of all manner of vehicles were on full beam. Trucks were plying as usual on this dirt road blowing up huge dust clouds. They reached Kandahar at about 3 am at night and were welcomed by Taleban authorities. All were put up in the guesthouse run by the Foreign Office in Kandahar. They had hardly settled in when they heard a loud explosion and some of them went outside with cameras looking to photograph the incident, but could not make out anything in the dark. Then they heard jets thundering overhead and some more explosions before the Azan (Call for prayer) of Fajr (Early Morning Prayer).

In the morning Mr. Tayyab political secretary to Mullah Omar came and took the delegation with him to see the bombed places. These were a dispensary and two houses. The dispensary had a large Red Crescent sign emblazoned on its roof and it housed about 50 patients at the time of the bombing, which occurred at exactly four thirty am in the morning. 11 patients were killed and a doctor was injured in this bombing. Two doctors and four nurses also lived on its premises. It was a large house, which was occupied by the Consul General of Pakistan in Kandahar before the attack[11]. The surgeon in charge of the dispensary Dr. Obaidullah told us that there were a large number of out-patients visiting the dispensary everyday before the bombing. The houses severely damaged next to the dispensary were owned by a Dubai based Afghan businessman quite advanced in age. He told us that he had come to Kandahar to settle down here and restart his old business. But now he was forced to abandon his plans

---

[11] I lived in the same house for about 3 months when civil works were going on at the flourmill site just outside the city.

because of this bombing. He had two of his brothers killed during the Russian campaign, now he was ready to die for his country fighting the Americans. He complained that these Americans were coward than the Russians because they come out at night to bomb the cities like thieves. He was itching to fight hand to hand if and when they send their ground forces to do battle.

Next day the delegation was taken to visit a place called Chokar Karaez, 80 kilometres from Kandahar. It was a greener area where people migrated from the city to avoid the indiscriminate bombing raids. Here about 10 families living close together were killed in a devastating raid. A 22 years old man told us that 19 of his family were killed in the bombing. He had a few acres of land here, which had a natural spring in it, where all of them worked. Out of the 19, 9 were women and 3 children. He also showed us a number of 4 feet long unexploded bombs which were lying by the roadside. Pictures of these bombs were published in some newspapers worldwide. 18 freshly made graves were shown to us in the graveyard nearby; in them they buried 3 to 5 persons each as it was impossible to bury them singly, because all the dead were in pieces and had to be collected to be buried.

Next the delegation went to see the main hospital of Kandahar called Mir Waiz Hospital. There the head of the hospital Dr. Bakht Ur Rehman Zakiri, whom the delegation met before touring its wards and corridors, told us that there was a severe shortage of life saving drugs, surgical instruments and blood for the seriously ill patients. He said those that who get injured are afraid to come to the hospitals, because hospitals are being targeted from the air on purpose. More than 100 patients died at two of them in Heraat and Kandahar recently, because of these air raids. The patients who cannot be treated here are sent to Quetta if they can make it, on a regular basis. In one ward a young boy (Falak Naz) in his late teens was under treatment for severe wounds sustained in the raid on the Red Crescent Dispensary described above. His uncle was looking after him and he told us that his younger sister was killed in the same raid. He worked as a mechanic's assistant in an auto workshop in the city centre. Falak Naz was in intense pain but could not speak because of his injuries.

Some delegation members also visited women's ward and there they met Sultan Bibi, a 60 years old woman who was also seriously injured. She was going to the market to buy groceries with her two daughters when suddenly bombs from the air fell and levelled the market, killing both her daughters. The woman attending her, who was a neighbour, told us that she has no relatives left anymore and was absolutely alone in this world. The delegation had a lengthy meeting with the Governor of Kandahar, Mullah Hasan, and discussed the pros and cons of the war. The gist of the talk he gave was that it is a war that the Taleban never wanted, but now that it has been imposed on them; the invaders will be defeated for sure. They will never be able to achieve their aims, he emphasized. They also met Wakil Ahmad Muttawakkil, the Foreign Minister of Afghanistan and asked him about the news in the Western press about his differences with Mullah Omar. He vehemently denied those reports as wishful thinking on the part of the West.

The delegation was allowed to meet anybody and go anywhere they liked without any restrictions, which was remarkable under the circumstances. On Friday, a normally closed holiday, shops were open and we found people busy in shopping. When the people saw delegation members walking in the markets they gathered round them and started raising slogans praising the Taleban and denigrating the invading forces. There was no animosity, just anger at what was being done to them. The people told us that the invading Russian Forces used to refrain from bombing the cities and population centres, but the

Americans are doing it deliberately, causing immense suffering for the people and intense hatred for this callous attitude.

In their discussions with the people far and wide, in and around Kandahar the delegation members found a remarkable amount of solidarity expressed by the people for the Taleban Government. There was talk of an all-encompassing national government without the Taleban in the press. The people laughed at this idea and said the Taleban are very much an integral part of the political landscape of Afghanistan; they cannot be ignored. When we talked to the Afghans about moderates and hardliners amongst the Taleban, they told us that there is no such division. It is a concoction of the foreign political forces constructed by them sitting in their boardrooms in Pakistan and elsewhere. This conception has no truck with reality on ground. All those interested in finding out the truth will have to leave their climate controlled board rooms and come down to wallow in the sands & dust of Afghanistan countryside.

U. T. N

UTN (Ummah Tameer e Nau), which was set up to start an economic activity in Afghanistan to alleviate abject poverty there, was declared a terrorist organization by US/ UN authorities in November 2001. If Amnesty International (AI), Human Rights Watch (HRW) and International Committee of Red Cross (ICRC) are terrorist organizations then UTN is one too. UTN had nothing to do with terror of any kind, imagined or real. This declaration was most probably for political reasons plus the need to justify an assault on Afghanistan, for which there was no plausible reason available. The US Central Intelligence Agency (CIA) laid the groundwork for the investigation and subsequent declaration, and Pakistani Agencies went along, probably knowing that it was a scam. Pakistani Agencies did what they did because they had orders to follow, and all those working for the Agencies had jobs to keep. In the world of intelligence there is no such thing as a rule of law or legitimacy, because the Agencies are a law unto themselves. This is true for most of the countries of the world and Pakistan is no exception. UTN was a soft target and very easy to do what they liked with it. It was obvious to us, during the investigation that a decision has already been taken by the authorities to declare UTN a terrorist organization. They went through the exercise to give it some kind of legitimacy or to put up a show or to write a report after it, we do not know. It was funny at times and quite amusing to see perfectly normal looking men behave like stubborn children, who knew fully well that they are in the wrong but would not admit it. However, one cannot deny the fact that the art of institutional lying by governmental agencies is now fully developed and separating fact from fiction has become almost impossible.

UTN was conceived in early 2000 by a group of concerned citizens who wanted to do something about the deteriorating economic, social and S & T (Science and

Technology) situation in all Islamic countries. A decorated nuclear scientist and engineer of Pakistan who designed and constructed many nuclear facilities in Pakistan headed it. Others who gathered with him in Lahore that day were engineers, entrepreneurs and reputable businessmen running successful businesses. Just because UTN was headed by a nuclear scientist, does not mean that it was engaged in any kind of nuclear proliferation activity. However, this fact provided an excuse and an opportunity for the foreign investigating agencies like the CIA to label UTN as a front for some clandestine activities. As Providence would have it, the investigating agencies got a tailor made opportunity to add another feather to their cap and justify an insane attack on Afghanistan. The theme of a nuclear device for use in Afghanistan was fabricated, as it was, exactly what was needed at that time and the easiest to frighten the people with.

First of all, to even handle radioactive material one requires extensive training and sophisticated equipment, which was never available to the Taleban regime or Al Qaeda for that matter. There is not even an iota of evidence to suggest that it was ever provided to them by UTN. Besides, to make a so-called dirty nuclear bomb with Cobalt 60 and mix it with conventional explosives requires remote manipulators and other sophisticated handling and measuring devices to proceed. Such things were not even known to the Taleban and have never been discovered in Afghanistan. It would have been suicidal and foolish to do so on the part of UTN, thus no effort was ever made to assemble these devices. Spent fuel from a nuclear reactor can also be used to put together a dirty nuclear bomb. How can an insignificant NGO like UTN get its hands on spent nuclear fuel? And even if supposedly it obtained some, how will it be handled and where? So far no such facility has been discovered in Afghanistan after 10 years of occupation by COF. There never was a nuclear reactor in Afghanistan and the ones in Pakistan cannot be reached.

Another bogey floated in the press, just before the attack, was the use of Anthrax by Taleban against the invading forces. In this case they went a bit too far and all COF were vaccinated against Anthrax before entering Afghanistan. Now if you put two and two together you cannot but reach only one conclusion, i.e. the invaders were going to use this biological weapon in the Country. It was widely reported in the press at that time, and a real danger existed that it will be used as an experiment on the hapless people of Afghanistan, if nothing else. We could see that the ordinary Afghan was being treated as canon fodder from day one of the invasion. Thus to guard against just such an eventuality defensive measures against Nuclear, Biological and Chemical warfare were provided to them by UTN, to help minimize casualties. These are called NBCD measures in the military jargon. Some papers were seized from an uninhabited UTN office in Kabul by the invaders and touted as evidence of an offensive NBC weapons program for Taleban in offing. A copy of the documents seized can be seen at the end of the book as Appendix, "A". It is funny that these documents formed the basis for declaring UTN a terrorist organization. The grammatical and contextual mistakes have been left unabridged on purpose. These documents were prepared in a hurry at the last moment; there was no time for a second reading, hence the mistakes.

What we saw happening in front of our eyes at the time of the attack on Afghanistan was amazing, reprehensible and incomprehensible at the same time. How and why should an armed to the teeth man shoot live ammunition at a child holding a toy gun: Coalition Forces attacking Afghanistan?

UTN knew that if she addresses the trigger happy armed man to deter him he will shoot her too, so she did the only sensible thing to do under the circumstances, she told the child to duck and take cover. Any sane and caring person will do the same in such a situation. This is exactly what UTN is guilty of, telling the child to take cover. UTN was in an unenviable position to further the capacity building program in Afghanistan and start sustainable economic activity for alleviation of poverty in the Country. What could be done easily at that time for USD 1/-, because of zero corruption, peace and security is now being projected @ USD 100/-. In many ways wheel is being reinvented at a huge cost. All UTN members were Western educated; no one came from a Madrassah or had any links to any Jihadi organization. It was a humanitarian organization on the lines of ICRC, HRW or AI. Its motto was: Help to build; build to help. And that is exactly what it tried to achieve, up to the last moment.

Islam means peace and it stands for peace, any deviations are circumstantial and must not be taken for granted, as being Islamic values. Demonization of Islam and Muslims in the Western media has gone too far. It is affecting circles where it was unheard of previously. A judge in New Zealand had a Maori Muslim woman removed from the public gallery in his court because she wore a head covering. He later apologized for his behaviour[12]. Would he have done the same to a catholic nun, if she entered his court? The answer is no, although she keeps her head covered too. These suspicions are fomented and strengthened by such actions as were taken against UTN. Blunting the good work being done by UTN in Afghanistan was a self-defeating exercise and such actions are wasteful of time and resources. One can argue that these are short term clever policies but they are not wise; in the long run they will backfire and come back to haunt those formulating them now.

---

[11] By Marty Sharpe and Paul Easton. *The Dominion Post*, 03 September, 2009.

George Tenet, in his book, claims that blunting UTN's building efforts in Afghanistan was one of his singular achievements[13]. It was a dubious achievement at best, not a singular one. Granted, Sultan and Chaudhry met Osama Bin Laden, but other members of UTN had no knowledge of that meeting. The talk about shared extremist tendencies amongst UTN members in the same book is sheer nonsense. What was shared was the effort to bring about a technical and economic union of Afghanistan and Pakistan, for the mutual benefit of both the countries. The idea was to marry the natural resources and amicable governance in Afghanistan with technical knowhow and skilled manpower of Pakistan in a way to bring about this union. The reference to the book about *doomsday* by Sultan has been quoted out of context by Tenet[14]. In actual fact Sultan has written about the suddenness of the end of the world as we know it[15], in that he speculates about the possibility of an accidental nuclear explosion. This phenomenon of a sudden end has been described in all the Scriptures including the Qur'an.

I remember noticing a dark blue coloured Range Rover SUV parked by the roadside not far from UTN's Islamabad office in July of 2001, i.e. much before the attack on Afghanistan or 9/11. It was obvious that these were CIA agents watching over us. We could not care less, since we had nothing to hide. The SUV had dark tainted glasses, but still we managed to catch a glimpse or two of its occupants.

---

[13] *At the Center of the Storm* by George Tenet with Bill Harlow, 268. Harper Collins, 2007, 1st edition.

[14] Ibid. 262.

[15] Sultan Bashir Mahood, *Doomsday and Life after Death*: "It will be a sudden event-----It may be a collision with a meteorite or may even be initiated by some catastrophic man-made devices such as sudden detonation of a large number of nuclear bombs by accident_", 89. Darul Hikmat International, Islamabad, 1987.

There were 3 of them and one was a woman, at times. Our only mistake is that we did not invite them for a chat and a cup of coffee in our office. During investigations the CIA interrogators used a lie detector and put Sultan and some of his colleagues on it. He promptly went to sleep while hooked to the polygraph and under questioning. The same questions were repeated over and over again and Sultan found it so boring that he resorted to snoring in the middle of the session. They used to wake him up and start all over again. They were trying to prove to the Pakistani intelligence officials present during interrogations that UTN was a front for some nefarious activities, like production of nuclear and other weapons for the Taleban. It was a dismal failure, because Sultan and all the others hooked to a lie detector responded to all questions asked with same answers without any deviations. They were speaking the truth; there were no lies to detect.

There was no fireside chat between Sultan and Osama Bin Laden in which any kind of WMD was proposed to be fabricated by UTN[16]. All that happened was that he advised Osama that such a project was not even remotely possible in Afghanistan. He spelled it out for them as to *why* it was not possible and they seemed to be convinced. This transpired when Osama was living near Kandahar airport in August of 2001, on the outskirts of the city. The statement in the book about a canister containing fissile material being shown to Sultan is humbug[17]. In fact Sultan told him that it took Pakistan 20 years to build a first generation nuclear weapon with the full backing of the GOP and there was nothing in Afghanistan for such a job to be accomplished. He tried to deter him from such an

---

[16] Tenet, *op. cit.*. 264.

[17] Ibid, "According to the account, an unidentified senior al-Qa'ida leader displayed a canister for the visitors that may or may not—the account was frustratingly vague—have contained some kind of nuclear material". 268.

undertaking and asked him to fund technical education rehabilitation in Afghanistan for gainful employment, instead. Osama Bin Laden said that he had no money to do that as all his funds have been frozen.

The other canard in the book is about Musa Kusa of Libya, in which he claims that Sultan offered him nuclear technology in return for money[18]. In fact Musa Kusa, working in the Libyan embassy in Islamabad at that time, contacted Sultan through a Saudi intermediary, to sound him out, and he gave him the same sound advice (like the Egyptian described next) to go for de-salination of seawater using nuclear energy generated heat. We now know that the Saudi chap was working for the CIA. Sultan was surprised at that time at his lavish lifestyle and used to wonder at the source of income of this thirtyish looking Saudi guy. It is revealing to note the anguish felt by the DCI if Pakistani scientists talk about peaceful uses of nuclear technology for progress and the absence of it, if Israeli scientists develop and use the same technology for a massive nuclear weapons build up.

In April 2000 CIA mounted a sting operation from Egypt and Dubai to involve and nab Sultan, after he successfully built and launched 2 reactors at Khushab and retired from PAEC. He got a call from Egypt from someone posing as a concerned scientist who was working for an organization trying to develop and adopt nuclear technology for power generation and other peaceful purposes throughout the Muslim countries. He offered him a consultant's position for a sum of USD 800/- per day. A meeting was set up in Dubai and Sultan embarked on a fully paid for trip. He was received and put up in a posh hotel for the night. In the meeting next day the Egyptian asked Sultan to replicate the Khushab design and build a similar reactor in Saudi Arabia

---

[18] Ibid. 263

for his organization. Sultan told him that it was not possible and asked him to give his requirements instead, and the parameters he wanted to work into the design. He also advised him to think about using nuclear technology for desalination to make water for drinking and irrigation. He agreed to consult and call back in a few days. The meeting over, Sultan came back to Pakistan. The call was made and Sultan sketched out a design to be used for desalination of seawater. Another meeting was arranged in Dubai and this time he was received and escorted by 2 Americans posing as investors in the venture. This time the hotel accommodation provided was even more upscale. They also demanded that he replicate the Khushab design for them. He refused and they supposedly became agitated and angry on his refusal. They then left him to think over it through the night, as the money they were offering was beyond anybody's imagination. Sultan called a nephew of his living in Dubai at that time, after they left and moved out of the hotel, coming back to Pakistan the next day. He saw through the game being played by CIA operatives; thus the sting operation flopped.

An American criminologist Todd Clear wrote in *New York Times* about tough laws promulgated in the US to control crime; "Tougher is Dumber" he writes, harsher sentencing has added more than a million people to an already burgeoning prison population of the United States. Tough laws and more police cannot/ will not control crime. The sources from which crime flows are different. He points out that, "About 70% of prison population of New York comes from 8 neighbourhoods of New York City and all suffer from extreme poverty, marginalization, exclusion and despair. All these things nourish crime[19]. Those holding political power in the US (and indeed elsewhere) have a common trait.

---

[19] Zinn, Howard, *A People's History of the United States*, 647. Harper Perennial, 2005.

They seek to keep their grip on power by diverting the anger of their citizens to groups of people who do not have the resources to defend themselves (like UTN). H. L Mencken an eminent social critic of the 1920's puts it succinctly; "The whole aim of practical politics is to keep the populace alarmed by menacing it with an endless series of hobgoblins, all of them imaginary[20]." The current such hobgoblins include: terrorism of al Qaeda, Pakistan, Iraq, Afghanistan, Islam and some more. By turning attention to them, by inventing or exaggerating their dangers, the failures of the American system could be concealed. Intelligence Agencies play a key role in inventing and then nourishing these otherworldly beings for politicians to exploit.

The agencies (mainly CIA and FBI) took away all the books, documents, hard disks and CPU's in use in UTN's offices in Islamabad, Kabul and Lahore. They pored over them for a couple of months and found nothing even remotely suspicious. They, then started resorting to concoctions, some of which have been described earlier, based on what they had gleaned from UTN's papers. All the stuff taken was returned unharmed as it is; it is still available and will be provided to anybody who desires to do research to get at the truth of the matter. In case of Sultan it was an assumption that since he is a nuclear reactor engineer (UK educated) and a practicing Muslim he poses a threat to U.S interests in the region. Besides he was advising the Taleban Government to be careful in dealing with and signing contracts with US and Europe based companies. For example a U.S company offered to install telephone exchanges in the Country for a sum of 15 million US dollars. The Taleban Communications Minister consulted Sultan for advice as to their suitability and price; obviously these exchanges were urgently needed. He

---

[20] Ibid.

advised them that the same job can be done for $ 5 million with Pakistan's help, saving 10 million dollars in the short term. There will be savings of millions more in the years to come when they run and maintain these exchanges themselves with expertise and spares available from Pakistan.

The same Communications minister for installation of these exchanges had made a request from Pakistan earlier. This was carried by Sultan to Islamabad, and he discussed it with the management of PTCL (Pakistan Telecommunication Company Limited). They did not take any interest in it, in spite of the fact that PTCL's network had been extended to all Afghan urban centres, like Kabul, Heraat, Kandahar etc. by rural telephony. It would have been very easy for PTCL to capture this market, both for land line telephones and mobile networks. Later a Chinese mobile phone company took the lead and installed the first mobile phone network in the Country in 2001. After that several other companies from France, Germany and India launched their networks and are working to this day. PTCL, the most likely and suitable company for the job is out of the market for good.

Afghanistan is the richest country of the world where the poorest of the world live. It has everything: topography, fertile soil, unexploited mineral resources, unexplored mines, not surveyed oil and gas fields and a hard working workforce. All that is required is to put it all together to bring it to fruition. The industrial base of the country was destroyed by the Russians before they left. Almost every industrial manufacturing unit was deliberately targeted and damaged or destroyed by them. We went through quite a few feasibility reports prepared by the Russians and some Western nations in detail. The possibilities we saw were enormous; not only for the country but for the whole region.

In 2001 there was a move by the then Government of Pakistan to impose heavy fines or confiscate properties of commercial and industrial tax defaulters. When push came to shove many of them decided to migrate to USA or Canada. Both these embassies set up offices in F-8/4 sector of Islamabad to facilitate and accelerate visa process for such applicants. They were migrating flush with cash, after selling out here, to go and set up their own businesses there. According to one survey by a news agency about 100,000 businessmen left the country taking with them more than 4 billion US dollars, in that year alone. However on reaching the promising shores they were shocked to discover that markets there were dominated and monopolized by huge corporations and multinational companies. Penetration was next to impossible, thus most of them decided to come back. They then discovered to their dismay that bringing money into USA is easy but taking it out is another matter. A paltry sum of 1000 dollars going out can trigger a vigorous investigation. Most of them were thus stuck between the devil and the blue sea, wasting all those dollars in the process.

Had these people known or cared to know the endless and lucrative opportunities in the neighbouring country it might have been a different story. Negative propaganda about Afghanistan in the western press also played its part. Business people were scared by all sorts of dire warnings about safety of capital, unreliability of the present regime, dacoits/ theft and lack of women's rights etc. An effort was launched by UTN to educate the people about the real situation on ground. Seminars, lectures and workshops were conducted and we arranged tours for anybody who was interested. We were surprised to discover the amount of effect this negativity had on peoples' perception about realities on ground in Afghanistan. However, those who ventured to discover and see for themselves ground realities during 2000 and 2001, before the attack, were equally surprised if not more. The welcoming atmosphere, zero corruption, no significant taxes, the prevailing safety and security, openness and forthright behaviour of the Taleban authorities was refreshing. Our offices in Kabul and Kandahar conducted these tours and mostly Suhail accompanied them where ever they went or wanted to go. There were no 'no go' areas in all Afghanistan during that time, even defence related establishments were approachable with little or no protocol. These tours were having a salutary effect on the people who visited; they came back as best ambassadors and advocates for investment in Afghanistan.

Cost of a unit of electrical power for industrial use was Rs. 2.50, compared to 5 in Pakistan, at that time. Power was available for 18 hours daily in Kandahar. Damaged grid stations were being run at maximum proficiency by old and experienced engineers under the supervision of Taleban Director Generals who had no knowledge of electricity. The working relations were remarkable and amazingly cordial under the circumstances. In most cases the engineers drew a better salary than their D.G's, supposedly supervising them. I visited the power distribution centre of Kandahar several times and never found anybody on idle, as is the norm in Pakistan. Innovation was order of the day. These engineers handled all technical matters; only administration was left to the non-technical Taleban authorities. Average salary of these engineers was 700 to 800 Rupees per month, which was very low and difficult to live by.

Taleban introduced an innovative scheme to ameliorate this situation; whenever output electric power increased from any facility they set aside Rs. 1/- per unit increase for welfare of the staff. This resulted in free meals at lunchtime and financial support on occasions, such as marriages etc. Maulvi Ahmad Jan, Minister for water & power related an incident to us about the time when he was in charge of Industries & Mines. There is a cement plant near Pul-e-Khumri, which was running at a very low capacity, producing 50 bags instead of 500 that it was designed for. The staff there did not like the Taleban Government and said so, thus they went slow and made excuses when asked to increase production. Mullah Omar advised him to give the staff one Rupee per bag produced above 50. This did the trick and production increased to 400 bags per day. It was obvious that Taleban meant what they said; even those opposed to them believed that much.

UTN was engaged in minimizing non-combatant casualties in Afghanistan up to the last moment. It was a gigantic task and beyond our capacity; we thus appealed to all the people who had some humanity left in them to come forward and help. Medicines were donated by some concerned people and caring organizations. I hand carried these with me on 07 October 2001 to Kandahar, a day before the attack. Very few Pakistanis were left there at that time and locals were also leaving for the mountains, thought to be safer than the cities. Hospitals were desperate for medical supplies like syringes, cotton, crepe bandages, glucose etc. It so happened that I had all those things in about 4 or 5 cartons that I could carry. The dispensary staffs were more than glad to receive these and looked visibly relieved. Supplies were also sent to Kabul and from there to other cities.

There was a grave danger of use of chemical and biological weapons by the attacking forces on population centres, because of lack of legitimate military targets. We warned the Taleban authorities about these dangers and damage control measures to be taken in such an eventuality. They were concerned but not overly worried about these weapons. This was intriguing to us and we probed and coaxed many for a plausible explanation. And we found that the Russians had used before these weapons in Afghanistan, but the terrain is such that it offers natural defences against these. These weapons release deadly heavier than air gases, which settle down after release from the aircraft. But people mostly move up into the mountains when seeking safety in Afghanistan, as it is a mountainous country. We however advised them to keep themselves covered at all times, drink lot of water and use a wet clothe or towel to cover face and mouth if such an attack is reported. There were no instruments with the Taleban to detect an attack by these weapons, but they had a sixth sense developed by past experience and they could tell by changing coloration, faintest of smells and cloud formation that chemical weapons have been released. Another danger was the use of FAE (fuel air explosive) and thermobaric bombs, which ignited everything in an area as wide as a football field. All oxygen gets consumed, a vacuum is created, a pressure wave is generated as air rushes in, for about 5 minutes nothing can breathe in there and lungs collapse, killing all living things. These weapons are effective against enemy hiding in caves and deep dungeons in an uneven landscape, like in Afghanistan. The best defence against these weapons is to run away as far and as fast as possible.

In January of 2002 various teams belonging to UN and some other organizations descended on Kandahar as indeed elsewhere in the country to clear unexploded ordnance and mines. In March 2002 a 4 feet long dud bomb was discovered and removed from the flourmill premises. It was lying next to the main building on the wet side of the milling operation, where wheat is washed and fertilized water drains out. We were using this water to irrigate vegetable planted plots and fruit trees. We did not know about this dangerous cargo dropped on us courtesy of COF forces. Had this thing exploded about 50% of installed machinery would have been destroyed. We were amazed as to how these people knew about unexploded ordnance lying hidden and almost buried in the ground. They carried it at the back of the mill in the hills about one km away and exploded it. The people entrusted with clearing these mines and other explosives apparently were well trained and knew their job. There never were any fatalities, only minor incidents that we heard about during these dangerous operations.

A BRUSH WITH INTELLIGENCE AGENCIES

On 23rd March 1999 President of Pakistan awarded Sitara e Imtiaz to Sultan for his meritorious services and singular achievements in design and development work in nuclear sciences for peaceful purposes. He conceived and founded UTN with the help of some of his colleagues and other like-minded people after his retirement from Pakistan Atomic Energy Commission in early 2000. The sole purpose of this non-governmental organization was development and generating economic activity for sustainable employment in Afghanistan. Towards that end multi faceted projects were surveyed, studied and analyzed. Actual work had started on some, while others were still under critical scrutiny when Afghanistan was attacked by a coalition of US, NATO and ISAF forces. On 23rd October 2001 he was kidnapped by our Intelligence Agencies from near Daewoo Bus Stop in Lahore and brought to Islamabad for questioning by the CIA and FBI. Dr. Chaudhry, a colleague of his, was also picked up by the Agencies in Islamabad for questioning.

On 26th of October, 2001 Pakistan Foreign Office spokesman announced to the press that these scientists have neither been arrested nor detained. On 28th of October, 2001 he was sent home by the detaining agencies and it was announced by the then Minister of Interior, Lt. Gen. Moeen Ud Din Haider and Pakistan Army Spokesperson, Maj. Gen. Rashid Qureshi that he has been released, as he is above board. He was, however again arrested the same day. On 29th of October, 2001 it was reported in the press that he has been handed over to CIA and FBI teams for interrogation about this activities in Afghanistan. On 30th October 2001 it was announced by The Army Spokesman that he is not under arrest and definitely not handed over to CIA etc. for questioning. He also emphasized that Sultan had never worked in any nuclear weapons programme of the PAEC and thus absolved of any wrongdoing. On 31st October 2001 it was reported that Sultan has suffered a heart attack and shifted to AFIC (Armed Forces Institute of Cardiology). On 1st November 2001 the family members of Sultan appealed to the President of Pakistan at that time, Gen. Pervez Musharaff to release him for health reasons as he was innocent and was being harassed unnecessarily. All this was reported by The Herald monthly of Karachi in its November 2001 issue.

On 11 November 2001 I was kidnapped by Intelligence Bureau (I.B) agents on the behest of American CIA and FBI. Agents of both these US Intelligence Agencies were stationed in Islamabad, as indeed elsewhere throughout the world. My kidnappers kept telling me that a senior Pakistani official (Additional Secretary) wanted to talk to me in confidence. I found it very funny that he had to send an SUV with 7-armed men to get me to talk to him. He knew very well where and how I lived, so it was so easy for them to get to me (or get me). I was going for Isha prayers (the last of the five daily ones) to the mosque when they picked me up. One of the goons inside brought out a mask to put over my head, but the officer sitting in the front prevented that. I later found out that he had a liking for religious people who were practicing Muslims. The vehicle was closed on all sides with black paper on windows to prevent one from looking out. I was taken to one of their safe/ guesthouses in Chaklala Scheme 3 in Rawalpindi and ushered in a well-furnished comfortable room to spend the night. Fortunately, I had a mobile phone on me and used it to call home to tell my wife as to what had happened. She was agitated to say the least and subsequently spent many sleepless nights up until my release after 33 days of incarceration.

I was not expecting this kind of treatment at the hands of our intelligence agencies. Before this incident articles started appearing in unknown (yellow) newspapers about me and other associates who were active in humanitarian work in Afghanistan since 1999. Some friends told me about it, but I ignored it as being irrelevant to me and a waste of time and effort for anybody indulging in such schemes. The details given in these stories were almost all outright lies and fabrications, e.g. I was supposed be a retired Brigadier from the Pakistan Army according to these stories. It was an obvious attempt to scare me: they wanted to see if I would get scared and take flight.

I did not have the time to read those stories in whatever newspaper they appeared in, besides I had not even heard of those papers which published all that rubbish. However, the offshoot was this kidnapping on 11th of November 2001. They kept me there for about 3 days and brought me clothes and other stuff from home which I needed for living. I knew they were watching me from a distance to see if I was distraught or not. They must have been disappointed as on the 4th day I told them in the morning that some utilities bills were pending at home and are due to be paid, and I have never defaulted on these bills ever. They seemed relieved, for anyone whose mind is agitated will not remember such small details; I felt a change in their attitude from that day onwards. Besides I slept soundly at night, ate well and did calisthenics inside the wide room. They promised to arrange payments on time and were convinced from that day (4th day) onwards that my kidnapping was a mistake.

They however kept me in various guesthouses of theirs for another 29 days, because obviously CIA and FBI insisted on it, as they were calling the shots, supervising our Agencies. My major concern was Ramadan and fasting with prayers in mosque (with Taraveeh), which I had not missed for the last 25 years. I cried and insisted so forcefully on it that they had sent 2 senior I.B officials (one a doctor) to apologize and cool me down. The tone and manner of these officials convinced me that they were helpless; they wanted to allow me more freedom in Ramadan but could not. I, thus decided to go along and see it through, as I was sure they will have to let me go sooner than later. They had nothing on me; it was a complete waste of time, their energies could have been better spent on pursuing legitimate targets, but in intelligence matters such comedy of errors is a common occurrence. I used to set the menu for the day every day and newspapers were provided regularly. Sometimes it felt like an all expense paid holiday, except for the fact that I could not go out for a walk. However, I was able to go for Friday prayers twice, during these 33 days of captivity, accompanied by I.B officials, of course. Since it was the month of Ramadan I became the Imam for the usual prayers and Taraveeh, in whichever guesthouse I was in. My followers (Muqtadeeh: those who stood behind in lines to pray) on these occasions were the staff manning those guest houses. Some of them were from the Army (MODC) and became quite friendly as time passed.

I heard quite a few anecdotes from the staff while staying with them. One recent incident narrated to me was about a Pak Army Major who was caught spying for Iran in Quetta. He belonged to the predominant sect inhabiting Iran and was under interrogation/ investigation; being kept and guarded in a Safe House in Quetta. The investigation dragged on for about 2 months, and the articulate Major became well known and the staff developed a liking for him because of his friendly attitude and likeable manners. He thus started taking liberties and testing the limits up to which he could go without offending anyone. He was eventually able to make good his escape from their custody and went straight to Iran, before they could get to him. He was never heard of again. The whole episode may have been stage managed, you never know; that is how this intelligence business is conducted.

The officer assigned to handle me (case officer), now working for I.B, turned out to be a nice and balanced guy. He was from the Police Service and joined Intelligence service subsequently. We met almost on a daily basis and I used to hand him over a list of items to be purchased from the market or to be brought from home. He did those chores diligently and cheerfully. He was of the opinion that the present circumstances (of war on terror) will change; these scenarios are unnatural and unheard of in this region and cannot last long. People of Pakistan are resilient and have an amazing capacity to tolerate sheer injustice mixed with coercion, but there is a limit and that limit is approaching fast. All foreigners will eventually leave and things will revert to normal as before. All the bloodletting and chaos is because of these foreigners amongst us, peace will get a chance once they leave for good. Fox News and CNN contacted my wife at home several times for an interview, while I was enjoying the hospitality of our Intelligence community. She declined, and they left disappointed. In one of the guest houses in G-10/1 in Islamabad, I was told that Hasan Nawaz son of ex Prime Minister Nawaz Sharif was kept in the same room I was occupying now, before being flown out of Pakistan to join his father in exile in Saudi Arabia.

The only question/ answer session with a CIA agent was held at about 2 pm at night in K block of the Pakistan Secretariat in Islamabad. I was woken up after midnight from sound sleep after about 10 days or so of being held and asked to get ready. We drove in a large black sedan car and alighted in K block of Pak Secretariat, I knew from a previous visit. My handlers asked me to put on a mask over my eyes for appearances' sake, which I did and they guided me up the stairs into a waiting room. I was quite amused by the exercise and remember thinking that this intelligence business is very costly. If these Americans keep betting on wrong horses they will go bankrupt one day. They were spending so much on me, who knew nothing of any value to them, a total and sheer waste of time and resources. In the waiting room I met a very nervous staff officer sitting by the phones of various colours. The whole set up did not impress me at all; it was not very professionally done. Anyway after about half an hour I was ushered in a large room and sat down by the side of a Pakistani I.B official (Addl. Secretary?) in his fifties. He was quite pleasant but very cautious and spoke in measured tones. At the far end of the room sat the CIA chap with his face partially hidden.

The questioning seemed a bit silly to me from the start. Have I met Osama Bin Laden or Mullah Omar was one, any knowledge of their whereabouts was another. The answer to both questions: no. Have I been to USA, if yes, when; answer: yes 4 times, in 1992/ 93 and 98. Where else have I travelled he wanted to know. Answer: New York to Panama by road, Miami to Chile, Argentina, Uruguay, Brazil, Peru etc by plane and car, as far as the new world is concerned. He was posted in Panama in 1993, when I went there, he told me. All these tours were with Jamaat Tableegh[21] for sublime reasons and had nothing to do with the mundane nature of this world. That seemed to satisfy him and it was all over in one hour. Maybe they were trying to show their superiors that some action was taking place to get funds or awards; I have no idea. The questions were routine and were asked without any enthusiasm like a performance for cameras. I left with a feeling of a staged melodrama. One possible reason for such lukewarm questioning might be that he knew that I do not know anything of value. But since

---

[21] It is a worldwide movement which shuns violence, militancy and/ or controversy of any kind. It consists of lay volunteers who travel the world propagating the transient nature of this world and the permanence of the next. The growth is phenomenal because of simplicity of the message and sincerity of purpose.

they had picked me up, he had no other alternative but to go through the exercise.

To put up a flourmill of the size we did in Kandahar in 9 months was no joke. It reached production stage in record time under adverse circumstances, prevalent at that time. I never had the time to meet anybody or to indulge any other (futile) activity or discussion, except for those necessary for the work in hand. Getting to Kandahar and back to Quetta again was in itself an uphill task. And when you have to hand- carry small electronic components for fitting on the way in, and for repairs on the way out; it was a nightmare. I spent long hours explaining to half literate officials as to what these were and for what use, at the border crossing and airline personnel at Quetta airport. The I.B officials asked to see all our account books for an "audit" by the CIA and/ or FBI personnel. I called the accountant to bring all books for them to see. This was done and all books were handed over to them to have a look. These were returned after 3 days without any comment.

The same day I was told by my case officer that I was done with CIA and cleared. However, I had to be their guest for a few more days because FBI personnel also wanted to meet me. By this time about 25 days had passed from the day of my kidnapping. My biggest regret was that almost the whole month of Ramadan had gone by and I could not get to visit a mosque peaceably. After about 20 days I was provided with a telephone for calling home or where ever else. I learned later that a niece of mine called Gen. Musharaff, the President at that time, from my home and told him about the injustice and highhandedness of all that had happened. She was married to a first cousin of his and knew him well. Setting up a flourmill or working for humanitarian causes is no crime; he said to her and talked to the authority coordinating US agencies' activities in Pakistan. That's when the telephone was provided. Musharaff was being regularly briefed and coerced by the

DCI, George Tenet[22], but he seemed to believe more in his own good judgment. It has to be said that he forged a balanced approach between the two opposing views: that of the Americans (CIA) and that of the local agency (ISI). He never handed over Sultan and some others to the Americans despite intense pressure.

Questioning by the FBI was much more professionally done and was quite relevant to the situation on hand. I was taken to a house in G-7/1 area in Islamabad. This time there was no mask or anything. We just drove there in an unmarked white coloured Toyota and I sat down in an upper storey room for them to arrive. Two agents came in shortly afterwards, introduced themselves and took seats next to me. There were just the 3 of us, 2 FBI and myself. They were quite frank and came straight to the point.

Q. Why set up a flourmill in Afghanistan and not Pakistan?

A. There was no corruption or red tape in Afghanistan and hardly any taxes, duties, levies etc. Profit margins were substantial. In Pakistan it is a pain in the backside.

Q. The other projects you were working on: did they get off the ground, any of them?

A. No, not really. Planning was completed and some logistics assembled in Pakistan, when bombing started.

Q. Who was funding it all?

A. Friends and shareholders who saw and felt the need to do so, mainly due to humanitarian reasons.

---

[22] Tenet, *op. cit.* 267, 286.

That satisfied them and one of them said that he wanted to get on with his life and wished me to get on with mine. "I don't want to be here at all" he said.

The other one came up and said, "Had there been any doubts in our minds about your project in Kandahar, it would have been razed to the ground by now, the reason it has been left untouched is that you people are in the clear".

The interview was over in less than 30 minutes; we shook hands and they left. I admired their approach, short, brief and to the point. Maybe by that time they had realized that it was a mistake to pick me up and an error had been made, so they just wanted to get rid of me.

I was exonerated and sent home from their Chaklala guesthouse in a Suzuki car by a driver after 33 days, three days after my encounter with the FBI. I.B was most concerned and scared about reporting in the press. They asked me not to talk to them or give an interview, just before releasing me. I kept my word and never went to the press. In August of 2007 I wrote a letter to the President of Pakistan, but never posted it. It is reproduced at Appendix "B". I was advised against it by friends, as they thought it will not make any difference. It may result in negative fallout rather than a positive one, 'so you better forget it', they said. It is, however impossible to forget the injustice of it all, the high handedness, the arrogance of power derived from the office held and the callous attitude of the authorities. Sultan has been placed on Exit Control List (ECL), and some others on an invisible watch list. What a travesty of justice in broad daylight. Those who are killing unarmed women and children on a daily basis (the Coalition Forces) are supposed to be law abiding, while those who tried to save innocent civilians from being slaughtered by the invading forces pose a security risk. Apparently, The U.S and U.N authorities can get away with it for the time being.

In February 2009, 3 Australian soldiers deliberately killed 6 civilians including 5 children in a raid on a compound in Uruzgan province in Afghanistan. The shooting was carried out in plain sight with full knowledge of the shooters as to what they were doing. Charges brought against them are for manslaughter and dangerous conduct, instead of first degree murder. It is no doubt a farce to placate public opinion, as it has been reported in the press. It is not being revealed, but by all estimates, the 6th victim was a woman. There were no men in sight, Taleban or otherwise. So they decided to shoot an unarmed woman and 5 children with automatic rifles. Petitions in Australia are now flying around to drop even these lame duck charges. The Australian Chief of Army Staff is sticking to his guns so far and wants to proceed with the prosecution[23]. However there is not much hope of real justice under any circumstances. They all follow the US lead, which never really punish their military for any kind of gross misconduct. Be it My Lai massacre in Vietnam, Abu Ghraib prison atrocities in IrAl Qaeda, slaughter of civilian tribal chiefs in Somalia or torture of innocents in Bagram, Afghanistan and other secret prisons elsewhere.

The Pakistani intelligence agencies were far more understanding, knowledgeable and efficient in processing information in the local environment than their foreign counterparts, the reason being that they comprehend local dynamics and flow of things far more deeply than foreigners. Thus I could see and feel that I.B officials reached the same conclusion in about a week's time which took the U.S agencies more than 30 days to reach. The I.B people, on seeing that I was not rattled or hostile towards them on my shabby kidnapping by them, became quite friendly. My attention to minor details of the chores I had left

---

[23] Rod Mcguirk Associated Press, in Yahoo! News. 13 October, 2010.

undone, because of this incarceration, convinced them that I was innocent of any wrongdoing. They went through the exercise from then on, because they had orders to carry out.

I have a lingering feeling that the kidnapping episode would not have occurred, if solely Pakistani agencies were entrusted with the job. These agencies are quite capable, willing and qualified to handle such situations. They are comparable to any intelligence agency in the world in their work and far superior in the local scenarios/ conditions for obvious reasons. It is a grave mistake to allow foreign intelligence agencies to run amuck in Pakistan. Such decisions undermine and compromise the good work done by our own agencies. As I experienced these foreign agencies come here with a pre planned political agenda; they are not after the truth by any stretch of imagination. Our decision makers have consistently failed to understand that most of our institutions (intelligence gathering is one) are far more capable than any foreign entity, because the understanding they bring to the job in hand will never be available to the foreigners. It has been reported in the press that in intelligence matters the Americans do not trust our agencies. It is impossible for any foreign intelligence agency to function effectively without active cooperation from our own. Thus the Americans have bought them out[24]; but buying into agencies like ISI does not always work. These press reports are either pressure tactics to bring them to toe the American line or published for public consumption. It is a monumental failure of weak, corrupt and severely compromised national leadership that allows foreign intelligence agencies a free hand in Pakistan.

Stereotyping by all Western intelligence agencies is quite common, as indeed it is with their media establishment.

---

[24] Bob Woodward, *Obama's War*, 4. Simon & Schuster UK Ltd. 2010

75% of this profiling is utterly false and political and they know it, 25% is unavoidable because of their lack of understanding of a complex situation and complacency in differentiating and deciphering the forces at work here. In my case they decided to conclude that I was designing triggering switches for a nuclear device by mixing it with conventional weapons, while working for UTN. The justification given, if one can call it that, was my electrical engineering background. I have been working on sound systems called SONAR and radio ranging and detection systems called RADAR, besides ship borne conventional weapon systems while in the Navy. Nuclear engineering is altogether a different piece of cake. I was never exposed to that nor had any formal training in that field. It is a ridiculous assumption that any electrical engineer can design or work on nuclear triggering devices without a lengthy and arduous training in a substantial nuclear facility. Those were self-serving fabrications and falsehoods being put out in the press, for political reasons. Even a cursory analysis of such propaganda will lead one to the truth. Nowadays, the top political leaders available to the world are so worthless that the people expect them to tell lies. A great deal of justification for these lies is being fed in the system by Western intelligence agencies.

Ridiculous stories about dirty nuclear bombs fabrication by mixing Cobalt 60 from gamma rays generator used in radiation therapy in nuclear medicine and extraction of Anthrax from infected animals were put out in the media in 2001. To mix nuclear fissile material with conventional weapons is not easy and it requires very sophisticated facilities to do so, as I have mentioned elsewhere in the book. Same is the case with Anthrax extraction; it requires constant purging of the lab atmosphere and sophisticated filters where this is taking place. Costs are in millions of dollars for even very basic facilities and it is next to impossible to hide from prying eyes. Of course, shameful torture facilities at Guantanamo, Bagram and secret detention centres around the world can produce any amount of "evidence" desired by detaining authorities from detainees there. But such *evidence* is not admissible in any court of law; that is the reason that none of these detainees has ever been tried in any neutral court of law. After the verdict in the case of Dr. Aafia Siddiqui, the Pakistani neuro scientist, it has been proven that U.S courts are more biased and unfair than the French Courts in 1753, when the French judicial system was inquisitorial, operated in private, and used torture[25] extensively to elicit confessions, the purpose being not to establish facts but confirm guilt[26].

Allegations against Sultan were various in 2001, after he was arrested by the Agencies. First allegation levelled was that he had contacts with Osama Bin Laden's Al Qaeda. Second was that the GOP was investigating his NGO namely UTN for any clandestine activity, as discussed earlier. The third was that as a nuclear scientist, he was not supposed to indulge in humanitarian efforts towards sustainable development in Afghanistan and try to save innocent civilians from being slaughtered by the NATO forces. All these charges were levelled by the GOP's official spokespersons and were later dropped, as there was no evidence to prove these. Any mention of CIA or FBI's involvement in these investigations was carefully avoided by all officials of the Government at that time.

There exists a natural tension between policy makers and intelligence providers, as most policymakers want intelligence to be tailored to their preferred policies. From

---

[25] There were two levels of torture, ordinary and extraordinary, that could be applied with or without a doctor present. Ian Davidson, *Voltaire in Exile: The Last Years, 1753-78* (London: Atlantic Books, 2004) 149. From the book "An Inquiry into the Culture of Power of the Subcontinent" by Ilhan Niaz (Islamabad: Alhamra Publishing, 2006) 207.

[26] Ibid.

early 80's onwards the CIA (under DCI: William Casey) decided to politicize intelligence analysis to please policymakers. Thus justification for huge defence spending was provided to President Reagan by exaggerating the Soviet threat. Twenty years later another DCI (George Tenet) decided to provide flawed intelligence to White House for attack on IrAl Qaeda and then Afghanistan. The issue of politicization of intelligence is not widely understood, but the problems it creates merit serious and concentrated action for its rectification[27]. "The CIA has committed every crime there is except rape," this was said by none other than General Walter Bedell Smith, a former DCI. The CIA has engaged in torture and abuse since the 1950's to support US policies[28].

On May 30, 2003 President George W. Bush said, "But for those who say that we haven't found the banned manufacturing devices or banned weapons, they're wrong, we found them." This statement gives a measure of lies and deceit employed to convince the American people for the need to go to war against Iraq. Those involved in this campaign, besides the president of the United States were the vice president, secretary of defence, national security advisor and various spokespersons of the US government. Their efforts to manipulate the American people are still not fully understood[29]. These lies and deceptions were central to the American Government's case for war. Afghanistan has been no different than Iraq. Same techniques have been applied and are being employed in Afghanistan to support a failed and aimless campaign going on there[30].

---

[27] Goodman, Melvin A. *Failure of Intelligence, Decline and Fall of CIA*, 13, 23. Rowman & Littlefield Publishers, Maryland, 2008.

[28] Ibid. 31, 47.

[29] Ibid. 225, 226.

[30] Woodward, *Op. Cit.* 207.

THE AFTERMATH

History of humankind is a history of human follies. It is amazing how nations forget lessons learned in the past through hard experience. It is very difficult to fight people who are not afraid of dying, as experienced by the Americans in Vietnam. If this lack of fear of dying is for religious reasons, it becomes all the more difficult to control, especially when you do not want to die yourself fighting such men. Machiavelli in 'Discourses,' alludes to this mindset and recommends using it to one's advantage[31]. Taleban are a religious lot, but they are not zealots. Very few of them are hardliners, but even these hardliners are prone to change and moderate their stand, given the right conditions. Most of them are middle of the road types and very human (in, *to err is human*, sense). One common trait we observed in their leaders was that they listen to you very attentively as long you talk sense to them. The moment you start talking at them they seemed to turn off. Tragedy is that the Taleban were never given a chance to explain themselves fully. Besides, whatever explanations they provided were not taken seriously and nobody cared to listen and understand what was being said.

Taleban do not necessarily believe in Osama Bin Laden's ideology per se. The predominant explanation we heard over and over again in Afghanistan from ordinary people was that 9/11 was an inside job carried out to get at Iraqi oil and establish permanent American presence in the oil rich Middle East. They asked for proof, when told to expel OSAMA BIN LADEN from Afghanistan, but it was never provided to them out of arrogance or ignorance or both. It is

---

[31] *The Discourses*, book 1, chapter xi, 103. Discourses upon the first ten books of Titus Livy by Niccolo Machiavelli. Bantam Books, Classics edition, 1981. Translated by Daniel Donno.

not easy to divide and rule the Taleban in Afghanistan. To make a precise distinction between moderate and hard line Taleban is very complicated: all of them are moderate on some issues and rigid in others, it all depends on who is doing the talking, where and when. Any faction that is cut out as being more amenable to whatever is the agenda of the occupation forces, is not *them;* it will not last long enough to bring about any significant or permanent change.

Taleban were aware of the fact that rule by men of religion in a country like Afghanistan, or indeed anywhere was contradictory to Islamic tradition in a sense. In that such men (Ulema) were expected to keep a moral distance from centres of worldly power, in order to maintain their influence over them to shape national policy whenever circumstances permitted. On the other hand they were forced to act and attain political power to fill a vacuum, which had been created after all foreign powers left, with the Russian withdrawal and complete chaos ensued. In another sense rule by men of religion is a reaffirmation of Islamic tradition. It is, however dangerous to tie the eternal interests of Islam to the fate of a transient ruler of this world. This attitude is reflected in popular suspicion of such men of religion; who play too prominent a role in the political affairs of any country; they are susceptible to corruptions of power and wealth like others before them[32].

Aftermath of the American occupation has been crippling for indigenous economic activity. Economic and financial

---

[32] "It could happen that at a certain stage of national development, the appeal of religious ideas- at least those sanctified by the cumulative tradition- would cease to have the same force as another set of ideas: a blend of social morality and law which was basically secular, but was related to general principles of social justice inherent in the Qur'an," Albert Hourani, *A History of the Arab Peoples*, 458. Harvard University Press, Cambridge, Massachusetts, 1991.

ruin is widespread, and there is no serious effort being made towards nation building. There is lot of talk about capacity building, but no concrete action. Wealth is being concentrated in very few hands in Afghanistan as a consequence of foreign occupation and the ensuing corruption. The people of Afghanistan need reforms now to improve their situation, not tomorrow or the day after. The present situation is ideal recruiting ground for all Jihadi organizations opposed to foreign occupation. Thus the Taleban will always win the numbers game as long as these circumstances prevail. Any increase (surge) in foreign troops will increase number of volunteers available to Taleban manifold. UTN was able to establish itself in Afghanistan by showing visible and quantifiable results, not words and promises, because it was set up as a non-governmental organization, in the private sector. It has been black listed for political reasons. It was done to kill two birds with one stone: remove UTN's hurdle impeding cheap exploitation of Afghan resources and discredit Sultan, albeit Pakistan's nuclear programme to slow it down. This is akin to destroying the Iraqi civil and military institutions after occupation and facing the fallout to this day.

One way to achieve quick and lasting reforms in Afghanistan is to rely on organizations like UTN to generate economic activity for sustainable development. Such humanitarian organizations, geared towards nation building, can bring the two peoples of both countries together for their mutual benefit. Sanity demands that an economic solution is pursued in Afghanistan instead of a military one. One achievable and desirable goal is to develop a minimum standard of living for the common man. At present almost 90% of the population is living below the poverty line. To combat that, a means of livelihood for most able-bodied persons of the country has to be found. This can be achieved by reviving all the projects that UTN was working on, as listed elsewhere. In a traditional Islamic society, like the one in Afghanistan, the endeavour should be to provide gainful employment to all able-bodied men. They will look after womenfolk, children and the old, as has been the practice in the Afghan society for centuries. All that talk about empowerment of women in Afghanistan is sheer nonsense. They already have enough power.

Another canard floated and being promoted by the occupation forces is the so-called Madam Democracy. It should be realized that democracy in South Asia is sexually transmitted; it is aptly called STD (sexually transmitted democracy). In India: Nehru then his progeny to this day, from1947 onwards. In Pakistan: Z A Bhutto then his immediate and extended family, from 1968 to this day. In Bangladesh: Mujib Ur Rehman then his daughter from 1972 to date. In Nepal: several Prime Ministers and top leaders from Koreala family to this day. In Sri Lanka: Bandaranaike and her family from 1965 and still continuing, off and on. It can be easily deduced that democracy as seen in the West is not suited to conditions in Afghanistan. This approach has been tried earlier, and failed miserably. The system of Loya Jirga works fine and everybody understands it. It is quite open and participatory as well, if worked on the right lines, by upright and honest men. It will be futile to impose STD on Afghanistan, because it will worsen an already bad situation. Even the non-sexual variety of democracy is not likely to take root, in this traditional society, where tradition goes back centuries and it is too deeply rooted to be stamped out by such imported ideas.

Anybody who has seen the proceedings in a Jirga will testify to its fairness, as long as it is convened and attended by the Mullicks. As reported by Sir Herbert Edwardes, who arrived in Peshawar in 1847 as assistant to Henry Lawrence, British Commissioner, resident in Lahore in his *Lahore Political Diaries, vol. 43:* the Mullicks talked Pushtoo. The deliberate way in which each delivered his opinion, the expressive gestures with which they enforced it, and the courteous silence observed by all the rest while one was speaking, was a model for any deliberative assembly[33]. Sir Edwardes later became Commissioner, resident in Peshawar. Sham democracy is now being peddled with the blessings of foreign forces, and it is the people who are suffering and bearing the brunt of this thinking. Afghan society is so traditional and conservative (primitive, in many ways), that to succeed one has to let tradition hold sway, be it Islamic or otherwise. That means, one has to let go and let them be. These people can and will progress at their own pace in good time. For the present the old and trusted Jirga system will suffice. They do not like things imposed on them in any way, from outside. As Bellow points out when mentioning remarkable similarities between the national character and customs of the Rajputs and Pathans: their rigid law of hospitality, the protection given to the refugee, the jealousy of female honour, the warlike spirit and insufferance of control, the pride of race, the jealousy of national honour and personal dignity, the spirit that loves to domineer, the reckless daring, the loyalty to the chief they trust, the love of sport, the readiness to take offence and quarrel among themselves when they find no enemy to give them employment[34], is at play in Afghanistan even today. They can only be helped by starting economic, income generating activities throughout the Country. But for that to happen, corruption has to be tackled first[35].

Corruption was almost completely eliminated by the Taleban. A culture of unmitigated integrity had taken root. In our dealings with public office holders, we got used to

---

[33] Sir Olaf Caroe, Chapter xxiv, Waziristan notes, 455. *The Pathans*. Oxford University Press, 10th impression, 1999.

[34] Ibid. 87.

[35] "Corruption is just like snow
It falls on the cliffs of the hills
And melts down below." Khalil Ahmad, *op. cit.*

hearing their tales of woe *after* completion of whatever chore was on hand, not *before* (as is the norm in Pakistan). It was a common refrain and quite true, as the cruel sanctions and embargoes were hurting the poor the most. As always, these sanctions were hurting the lowly officials the most, although the Taleban high ups were not immune to this punishment. These low ranking officials accepted any tips (baksheesh) given by us with caution, grace and gratefulness. There was no haggling or bargaining of any kind and repetition was also not necessary or required. Any money that changed hands was really like a tip and nothing more. However, we used to give it another meaning by our way of thinking and the Pakistani background (upbringing, if you like). We thought that this practice would facilitate our dealings with the office holder in the future; but the official concerned had no such thoughts; he was only grateful (because of extreme need) and a little afraid too. The punishment for such petty crimes was swift and severe: the official could loose his precious job if reported against. A corruption free environment is a boon for any kind of business enterprise and we could see that the Taleban regime was also aware of this fact.

We could see that slowly but surely, this realization was settling in and more and more people from across the world were being attracted to this phenomenon. That is where funding for UTN was coming from: complete strangers would call or walk in to make an investment or a donation, as the case maybe. Sincerity and honesty of purpose of the Taleban Government had started to pay dividends, and we were in position to reap the benefits as they grew. The people who trusted us with their money, really and actually trusted the Taleban. Our trustworthiness was based on this confidence by the people in *them* and our association with *them*. It was a strange situation we found ourselves in and fretted a lot about it. We had to find ways to live up to the expectations of these investors and the Taleban Government. It was not an easy job, but it was a heady medicine to contend with and job satisfaction it brought with it was tremendous.

CIA has now been implicated in drug trade as per an article in New York Times in October 2009[36]. As reported in that newspaper, they have been paying huge sums for the last 8 years to Ahmad Wali Karzai brother of the President of Afghanistan, the biggest drug dealer in Afghanistan[37]. Other warlords and drug smugglers are also on their payroll. It is interesting to note that wherever CIA sets up shop, drug trafficking rises exponentially. It happened in Vietnam, Colombia, Iran, IrAl Qaeda and now Afghanistan. George Tenet laments about shortage of funds for CIA in his book[38]. This shortage may have been made up by aiding and abetting the drug trade. For an organization like the CIA drug trade is lucrative, easy and can render huge profits. It could also provide a fertile ground for recruiting the *right* kind of people to work their tradecraft.

These agencies have a lot of coercive power at their disposal, because of the money that they have and political backing. However, men like Osama Bin Laden and his cohorts pose a problem because they shoot back. It is not easy to assassinate them and now it has been proven, very difficult to find them, even with an Intelligence Industry of USD 80 billion. So to compensate for these shortcomings and failures, these intelligence agencies might have decided to deal with the softest of targets first, in order to show some progress and justify the huge expenditure being incurred on them by the taxpayer. What could be softer than an NGO like UTN (and those who were managing it)? It was a misguided operation and no attempt was ever

---

[36] Dexter Filkins, Mark Mazetti and James Risen in *New York Times*, 27 October, 2009.

[37] Woodward, *op. cit.* 66.

[38] George Tenet, *op. cit.* 14.

made at any stage to get at the truth of the matter. Such *intelligence* activity is very easy because these NGOs have no real power as they are run by ordinary concerned citizens who care and dare to uplift these children of a lesser god (the poor of the world) for whom nobody gives two hoots: a grave mistake under the circumstances.

It has now been confirmed that all U.S intelligence agencies operating in USA and worldwide use torture as standard operating procedure. If our experience with these agencies is any guide, it is tragic that most torture victims are absolutely innocent of any wrong doing. I give below a comparison between Dr. Aafia Siddiqui, a U.S/ Pakistani citizen and Ms Yvonne Ridley, a British one. Dr. Aafia, a neuroscientist who did her PhD from MIT, was apprehended by the largest Pakistani intelligence agency, ISI, along with her 3 children, in Karachi and handed over to CIA for interrogation. They took her to Bagram airbase detention centre (prison) near Kabul. Ms Ridley, a London based journalist working for the Sunday Express, tried to reach Kabul under cover just before the CIA sponsored bombing started, and fell off a donkey she was riding in Jalalabad[39]. That blew her cover, and she was arrested by Taleban authorities on spying charges. What happened to both women subsequent to their arrests is revealing and speaks volumes about the humanity of Taleban and bestiality of COF.

Dr. Aafia Siddiqui	Ms Yvonne Ridley
She was severely tortured.	Never tortured.
Held incommunicado for 6 years.	Held for just 10 days.
Given solitary confinement.	Not really confined.

---

[39] Hannah Bayman, *op. cit.* BBC News Online.

Her children were taken away.	Nothing was taken from her.
She was shot in the stomach by *valiant* CIA operatives.	Her life was never threatened.
She has been sentenced to 86 years in prison by a racist US Judge, and flawed U.S Justice system.	She went home after only 12 days in captivity.
She was so badly treated that she has almost lost her mind.	She embraced the faith of her captors, i.e. Islam, after release
She cried all the time in prison, but nobody came to her help for 5 years.	She argued with the Taleban and hung her panties to dry high up, for their recruits to see.
Charges brought against her are impossible to prove. All are based on hearsay.	Taleban pleaded with her to take her panties down from the high wire, when she refused, they escorted her back to freedom.
2 of her children, aged 3 and 5 at the time of her capture are still missing & presumed murdered in detention.	She missed the 10th birthday of her daughter by one week only.
She was treated with disdainful contempt and abused both physically and mentally in Bagram prison.	She was treated with due respect and addressed as 'sister' by Taleban.
If she lives and recovers from her mental and physical wounds, she is	She was so enamoured by the Taleban that she has become their best advocate

bound to hate the Americans forever.	& a fan.
She has been repeatedly strip searched by all US detaining authorities out of vengeance.	She was never even touched by the Taleban.

If one reads the above comparison between the lines, it will become clear what this war on terror is all about. It is a clash of two very different ways of life, one as practiced by the Taleban in Afghanistan and the other that of the invading forces. But one thing is clear and obvious: here are 2 approaches to succeed in a country and rally its people, which are poles apart; one is through the use of brute force and imposing their point of view on the people by the leaders; the other through humility, patience and by setting an example for people to follow. It is a David and Goliath struggle; history and Scriptures tell us that Davids of this world prevail in the end. The choice looming for the people of Afghanistan is between peace and tranquillity with poverty (Taleban) or chaos and corruption with riches (COF). The people of Afghanistan opted for the former, but the occupation forces want to impose the later on the hapless people. The foreign (imported) solution requires huge funds, large armies, murder and mayhem, to succeed. Whereas the Taleban model does not require any of these things; however to succeed they require to be left alone in Afghanistan without interference from outside, first and foremost. And that is what COF will not let them have, because if they did, they will succeed without any outside government help. That will be a triumph for the Taleban, and the likelihood of other nations following suit will increase.

Since the Americans want to impose their values and systems in both Afghanistan and Iraq, they require corrupt and compromised leaders to do their bidding. Honest and upright people like the Taleban with nationalist agendas, will not obey them and they will never be able to control them. Thus from the American perspective war was the only option. It is a war, which the people of Afghanistan or the Taleban never wanted. It has been imposed on them by US politicians. The war will end as soon as it becomes politically unsustainable, like in the USSR before it, which seems increasingly likely. However, the people of Afghanistan will have to go on sacrificing their well being, livelihood and life up to that point in time. The period most often quoted is about ten years for any occupying force to fail in Afghanistan, give or take a few years; we are in the tenth year now. The rest is easy arithmetic. It is a fact that the sacrifices being given by the Afghans increase an already steep price being paid by the invaders to stay. The more they sacrifice the harder it becomes for the occupying force to sustain itself in the Country. Bear in mind that the graph of this difficulty to stay climbs logarithmically when plotted against that of the sacrifices on offer. Thus the more an occupier stays in Afghanistan the harder it gets, as time piles on.

"There is the past and its continuing horrors: violence, war, prejudices against those who are different, outrageous monopolization of the good earth's resources by a few, political power in the hands of liars and murderers, the building of prisons instead of schools, the poisoning of the press and the entire culture by money. It is easy to become discouraged observing this, especially since this is what the press and television insists that we look at, and nothing more.[40]"

The above from a modern scholarly work by an eminent US professor is aptly put. However, the future may not be as blighted as the past has been. There is a growing revulsion

---

[40] Zinn, Howard, *op. cit. 687.*

against endless wars, deceit, spreading of lies, mindless torture, arrogance and misuse of political and financial power. People have started seeing through this charade. So there is hope, which is based on and nourished by the people's ability to bring about a change for the good of humanity at large. This *real* change is overdue and cannot be held in check for long now. Such a change would be upon us when organizations like UTN are allowed to pursue humanitarian development work anywhere in the world.

The US and other NATO countries start making the right kind of noises whenever Pakistan plays hardball. By Pakistan, the Armed Forces and Intelligence Establishment are meant. National political leadership does not count anymore. It is interesting to note that US authorities never refrain from promoting and foisting this leadership on the people of Pakistan although they probably know the depth of hatred felt for them by the populace. The reality is that the interest of Pakistan has never been at the heart of US policies towards Pakistan and it will never be. The kind of work UTN was involved in goes against the grain of this US policy, as it was in the interest of Pakistan and the region. The US and NATO countries dare not mess with Pakistan because of strategic reasons. If only our policy makers had vision and brains, this region's predicament could be different.

ENDGAME

It is imperative that a wooden handle is used on an iron-saw to cut wood itself. Without this handle the hands of the cutter will bleed. The COF has a stout handle at its disposal for now, for the cutting operation. Akbar, the great Mughal emperor tried his level best to control these tribal areas on the border between Pakistan and Afghanistan. He deployed his considerable armies here to do the job. However, in the scales of history the result was incommensurate with the effort put out. The might of Akbar had not prevailed in any decisive fashion against any of the tribes except those who found it to be in their interest, in return for consideration, to guard the King's highway[41]. The American exit from Afghanistan will most probably be chaotic and will once again leave them in a lurch, until the strongest takes control. But before they go they will damage almost every aspect of the Afghan society and the Country as a whole. Afghans have the ability to bounce back after an invasion or seeming occupation after years of experience with a succession of intruders. Their culture, traditions and values have proven to be far superior to those of any invading forces. Take for example their tradition of *nanawatai* (a deputation or entering in), by which once they give asylum (meaning shelter) to someone, it is against their *nang* (personal honour and pride), to give him up to anybody. In Afghan society *nang* is defended with life[42].

The possibility is steadily growing that U S and most of its allies will go bankrupt trying to find Osama Bin Laden and Mullah Omar in Afghanistan. What if they fail in the end? What will be the consequences, nobody knows exactly, but educated guesses abound. The finale to this episode is approaching fast and it may well be over sooner than later,

---

[41] Olaf Caroe, *op. cit.*, chapter xiv, 220.
[42] Ibid, 142, 369.

i.e. in a year or two. Guerrilla warfare cannot/ will not be won by technology alone. Ample proof of that came with the defeat of USA in Vietnam. Organized modern technology was used ruthlessly to crush organized human beings, savagery of which was never seen or heard before[43]. The human beings won hands down, and the technology floundered.

A new technique of employing civilian *contractors* to kill non-combatants is being employed by the COF. To hire soldiers of fortune for dirty jobs, like killing of civilians including women and children and kidnappings is a sign of weakness and a sure fire way to fail anywhere. For Afghans, like some other proud races, their women and children are sacred, and any harm coming to them makes them stark raving mad. Machiavelli talks about this in his classic 'The Prince'----" Still a prince should make himself feared in such a way that, though he does not gain love, he escapes hatred; for being feared but not hated go readily together. And this can only happen if he does not bring harm to their property and their women" (and children)[44]. Mountstuart Elphinstone, the first Ambassador (and a scholar) of Imperial Britain to the 'Kingdom of Caubul' in 1809, who came to know the Afghans intimately, talks about the character of Afghans thus: their vices are revenge, envy, avarice, rapacity and obstinacy; on the other hand, they are fond of liberty, faithful to their friends, kind to their dependants, hospitable, brave, hardy, frugal, laborious and prudent; they are less disposed than the nations in their neighbourhood to falsehood, intrigue and deceit[45]. Elphinstone was based in Peshawar and it was the seat of government of Afghanistan (Caubul) at that time.

---

[43] Zinn, Howard, *op. cit.* 469.

[44] Machiavelli, *The Prince, op. cit. 60.*

[45] Olaf Caroe, *op. cit.* 278.

For these reasons (of revenge) suicide attacks are likely to increase not decrease with time. These attacks are apparently becoming more sophisticated and penetrating with experience and after ten years no way has been found to stop them. Most probably these murdering civilian contractors will seriously jeopardize and harm the COF mission in Afghanistan, and will have to be withdrawn in the end. Many scandals have come to surface pointing towards the lawlessness of these hired contractors. Most famous of which is Black water, a company-selling mercenaries to kill and maim worldwide. It is being run by ex US military soldiers. Their main advantage to COF is that they are not governed by any law, national or international. Thus they can get away with murder and genocide in the name of security. They cannot be court martialled because they are technically civilians. Their main defence against any allegation of atrocities committed by them is that *it was in self-defence*. Since these mercenary contractors operate outside the jurisdiction of any law, it is very difficult to control them. And that probably will be their undoing in Afghanistan and elsewhere.

It is not being highlighted, or even being reported as to how many orphans and widows this stupid & brutal war has created in Afghanistan. But they must be in hundreds of thousands. To settle or even handle them is an enormous task, beyond the ability of the present Afghan set up. Also the set up in Afghanistan does not want to indulge in affaires that yield too little for them. Settling these unfortunate lost souls is not profitable for the corrupt. Thus there is an urgent need to arouse public awareness about the scale of the problem, worldwide. No Government will do it, so it is the responsibility of the media, both local and international, to take up their plight for redressel.

 Had the Americans not deliberately murdered the staff of Aljazeera Arabic channel, there may have been no

Aljazeera English now, beaming worldwide a non American (or anti American) point of view. The birth of English Channel of Aljazeera was hastened in response to the brutal and calculated killing of their Arabic language staff in Baghdad by a missile strike from the air. It has become immensely popular because of its realism and truthful reporting. This Aljazeera Arabic television was a thorn in the side of the American invading forces in IrAl Qaeda. They reported and showed the atrocities being committed by them in the name of freedom. So they decided to do something about it and targeted the offices of the satellite channel killing their staff[46]. It was a classic case of shooting the messenger, in desperation or avarice or both. It is abundantly clear that the champions of democracy care two hoots about it if the democratic dispensation is not pliant and supplicative.

Howard Zinn quotes in the first chapter of his book *A People's History of the United States:* "The cry of the poor is not always just, but if you do not listen to it, you will never know what justice is,[47]" is very ominous and true in case of Afghanistan. How is it that the world's poorest nation has been invaded by the richest, and there is no real opposition to it throughout the whole world? Granted OSAMA BIN LADEN was hiding there: but you don't kill, mutilate and brutalize the whole population of a Country for one man. Record of the United States is abysmal in such brutal assaults; a few glaring examples of brutalities committed are given below:

- The early colonists killed the Indians out of vengeance and frustration of not being able to live off the land as well as the Indians. They proceeded to slaughter them to prove their vain superiority over

---

[46] By Henry Michaels, 09 April, 2003 at wsws.org

[47] Zinn, Howard, *op. cit. 10.*

them; but that still did not grow much corn for them[48]. This is in the book *American Slavery, American Freedom* by Edmund Morgan.

- Out of an estimated population of 10 million indigenous Indians living north of Mexico at the time of arrival of the white man, only 300,000 were left when they were done with them, at the turn of the century. 90% of those who trusted and welcomed these strangers from far off shores were decimated in an unprecedented genocide for land[49].

- The last Indian massacre took place near Wounded Knee Creek in the last days of 1890, at Pine Ridge, South Dakota, just after Christmas. After their leader Sitting Bull was assassinated by Indian Police aided and abetted by US Government, 120 men and 230 women and children sought refuge at Pine Ridge. They were surrounded by U.S cavalry armed with Hotchkiss guns, with an effective range of 2 miles. Outnumbered and outgunned these Sioux Indians were butchered mercilessly. About 50 survived out of the original 350[50]. 25 US soldiers were also killed, due to *friendly fire*.

- In 1763 a British General, Jeffrey Amherst, ordered commander of Fort Pitts, to give the unsuspecting Indian Chiefs blankets from a smallpox hospital. This resulted in an epidemic amongst them, killing many. This was a pioneering effort at biological warfare[51] used by the British against the hapless Indians. Bear in mind that at that time negotiations were taking place between the two sides.

- By 1800 10 to 15 million black African slaves had been brought into America by slave traders. The

---

[48] Ibid. 25.
[49] Ibid. 16, 524.
[50] Ibid. 295, 524.
[51] Ibid. 87.

methods employed were such (abduction, jailing, packing below decks like fish, chaining) that 1/3rd of all slaves died en route[52]. So the actual abductions in Africa were to the tune of 45 million, men and women. Average age of the slaves was 30 years after they reached the American shores, because of diseases, pestilence and torture.

- In 1818, Andrew Jackson, a land speculator and the most virulent enemy of the Indians, ordered many Seminole Indian villages burned and their inhabitants killed in the Seminole wars against Spain. All this was done to cede Florida to the United States. Excuse given was that escaped black slaves from Southern cotton plantations were taking refuge in their villages in Florida[53]. Florida, at that time administered by Spain, was *sold* to the United States by her in 1819.

- The Mexican war was instigated by James Polk, U.S President and a Democrat, to annex California, New Mexico, Nevada, Arizona, Utah and part of Colorado from Mexico. It was started in May of 1846 and concluded in February 1848 by the treaty of Guadalupe Hidalago. All these territories were in Mexico, which won its independence from Spain in 1821 after a protracted war. The U.S coveted these areas; thus forced a war on the Mexicans and occupied them after horrible bloodshed and brutalities[54]. There were widespread desertions, rebellions and uprisings against their superiors by the rank and file of the attacking U.S Army. Discipline and morale was low throughout the campaign, resulting in rape, plunder, burning and

---

[52] Ibid. 28, 29.

[53] Ibid. 129.

[54] Ibid. 152 to 169.

pillaging of Mexican villages causing untold sufferings to those living there.

- Frederick Douglass, spoke on 4th of July celebrations, 1852. He was an ex- slave, and published his own newspaper *North Star* from Rochester[55]:

"What to American Slave is your 4th of July? To him your celebration is a sham; your boasted liberty an unholy license; your national greatness a swelling vanity; your sounds of rejoicing are empty and heartless; your denunciations of tyrants, brass-fronted impudence; your shouts of liberty and equality, hollow mockery; your prayers and hymns, your sermons and thanksgivings, with all your religious parade and solemnity, are to him mere bombast, fraud, deception, impiety and hypocrisy---- a thin veil to cover up crimes which would disgrace a nation of savages. There is not a nation of the earth guilty of practices more shocking and bloody than are the people of these United States at this very hour.

Go where you may, search where you will, roam through all the monarchies and despotisms of the Old World, travel through South America, search out every abuse and when you have found the last, lay your facts by the side of everyday practices of this nation, and you will say with me that, for revolting barbarity and shameless hypocrisy, America reigns without rival..."

- President McKinley took over Guam, Puerto Rico and Philippines from Spain in December of 1898 for a payment of $20 million. He said he got a message from God to take over Philippines. However, the Filipinos did not get that message and rose in revolt against American rule in February 1899. It took U.S

---

[55] Ibid. 182 – 83.

3 years and 70 thousand troops to put down this popular revolt. The conduct of the United States in this fighting is aptly described by a volunteer from Washington in a letter: "Our fighting blood was up, and we all wanted to kill 'niggers'. This, shooting of human beings beats rabbit hunting all to pieces[56]."

- More than 100,000 were killed in Hiroshima when a Uranium bomb was dropped on civilian population to test its effectiveness. Then a Plutonium bomb was dropped on Nagasaki, killing 50,000 civilians including American prisoners of war to check its effectiveness. It was known that Japan was prepared to surrender unconditionally, as the Japanese secret code had been broken and all their messages were being monitored; still these bombs were dropped to keep USSR out of Japan[57]. President of USA ordered this one and only full-scale nuclear attack on any country in the world.

- U.S army invaded North Korea as U.N army in July 1950 to uphold the *rule of law* against *rule of force* by the communist regime in the North. 2 million Koreans were killed on both sides, mostly by the U.S army and Air Force in 3 years of napalm and other incendiary bombings of North Korea. The 2 Koreas stand divided to this day at the 38th parallel, as just after 2nd world war and before the Korean War. This adventure, ordered by President Truman, had everything to do with *spheres of influence* and nothing with rule of law as implied by the U.S[58].

- From 1964 to 1972 the richest and most powerful nation in the world- the U.S, used latest military technology and most lethal weapons short of nuclear to beat into submission an impoverished peasant

---

[56] Ibid. 313, 315
[57] Ibid. 422-23-24.
[58] Ibid. 427-28

country- Vietnam and failed[59]. 2 million Vietnamese died in the process, most of them non- combatant women, children and the infirm.

- On March 16, 1968 a company of American soldiers went into the hamlet of My Lai 4 in Quang Ngai province in Vietnam, rounded up all inhabitants and shot them to death in cold blood. 500 people were killed, all were unarmed and 90% of them were women and children. They were then buried in 3 ditches on site[60]. Only Lt. William Calley was sentenced and incarcerated for a *grand* total of 3 years.

- From May 1964 to September 1969 25.000 deadly sorties were flown by U.S bombers to bomb defenceless and beautiful Plain of Jars in Laos. This was never reported in the mainstream media in the U.S. 75,000 tons of lethal bombs were dropped there, killing or wounding close to 100,000 people on ground without discrimination[61]. Reason for the bombing was to test new weapons and imperial hubris.

- More than 3 million Iraqi and Afghani civilians have been killed or wounded so far in the ongoing war on terror and there is no end in sight. About 10 million have been displaced and made homeless[62]. Depleted Uranium weapons, cluster bombs and land mines have been used freely by COF in both countries[63]. This has caused widespread diseases and a large population of maimed and disabled men women and children.

---

[59] Ibid. 469-70 *passim,* 473, 475, 477, 481, 485, 487, 502.

[60] Ibid. 478-79.

[61] Ibid. 481-82-83.

[62] Dr. Polya, Gideon, *op. cit.* 09 July, 2009

[63] Tripod.com. DU ammunition use in Gulf war, analysis.

The technique of lying to the people has been perfected over the years in the United States. It is a tragedy that the mainstream media in the US is so dishonest and controlled that 90% of its reporting is either outright lies or based on falsehoods. More and more people are now turning to alternate media (like the representative press) operating in the West and elsewhere. Despite the lies and propaganda by the Western press I heard and saw ordinary people in Afghanistan seeing through this façade of deceit. Although Afghanistan society is not *addicted* to reading newspapers or the like, however some propaganda did reach them, over the radio mostly. But they could easily pick out the lies and many jokes were spun around them. As experienced by the British in early 20th century, when they tried to pacify and set up some sort of *law and order* based on their system in NWFP in Pakistan, the current invaders are also facing the same problems. The most difficult of all situations is when they come armed with laws and regulations which had not necessarily, as seen by the people, any relevance whatever to the standards by which a Pathan society lived. A good example is the tradition of *Nanawatai and Melmastia.* These concepts and their connotations are unknown in the western society. Both are explained next.

As related by Sir Olaf in his historical work: the denial of sanctuary is impossible for one who would observe Pakhtu; it cannot be refused even to an enemy who makes an approach according to *Nanawatai* ___ a verbal noun carrying the meaning of 'coming in'. This is an extension of the idea of *Melmastia,* hospitality, in an extreme form, stepped up to the highest degree. Under *Nanawatai* a person who has a favour to ask goes to the tent or house of the man on whom it depends and refuses to sit on his carpet, or partake of his hospitality, until he shall grant the boon required. The honour of the party solicited will incur a stain if he does not grant the favour asked. The giving of hospitality to the guest is a national point of honour, so much so that reproach to an inhospitable man is that he is devoid of Pakhtu, a creature of contempt. It is the greatest of affronts to a Pathan to carry off his guest, and his indignation will be directed not against the guest who quits him but to the person who prevails on him to leave[64]. This, or something like it, was the reception accorded to the outlaw from British justice who fled to the hills. It should be clear to the invading forces (COF) by now that the culture they are in confrontation with is quite alien and not easily understood by them. This is just one example of the difficulties faced by the British Indian Government and a contributing factor towards the (relative) independence of the tribal areas. And the British Government took over from East India Company after 1857 war of independence. They could not control these areas, as they liked, in about hundred years that they were in control in the rest of India.

The British Government wanted to use these fiercely independent Pathan tribes as a buffer against Russian expansion towards the South. They failed for many reasons and one was that they adhered to a different religion. If they were Muslims like the tribes their task would have become easier. However, having said that it is also a fact that an Afghan (read Pathan) is an Afghan first and a Muslim later. But he will be more inclined to listen to a fellow Muslim than others. So far these tribes have been successfully guarding their anarchical freedom of 'Drai Mahsit"[65]. Pakistan was able to win them over after a lot of trials and errors and they became a formidable bulwark against any invasion from the North. It was this bulwark, which withstood and then defeated the USSR invading forces. That formation is being destroyed now by attacks being carried out by COF in these areas. Consequences of which will become apparent after foreign forces leave and Pakistan is left in the lurch to deal with the fallout. These same tribes were able to hold

[64] Olaf Caroe, *op. cit.* 351.

[65] Ibid. 398.

themselves and even advance in Kashmir against the Indian Army in 1948, after the partition of India in 1947.

EPILOGUE

The 80 billion dollar a year US Intelligence industry finally succeeded and sent US Navy SEALS to get the better of Osama bin Laden on 2 May, 2011, while this book was under publication. It cost the US taxpayer 1.3 trillion dollars to get the man[66]. Collateral damage amounted to one woman and three men, all unarmed, who were also gunned down. It took 10 years to get the job done. The whole episode reminds me of *Armon*[67] written at the end of his book by Sir Olaf Caroe. There are striking resemblances there. There are a dozen or so men of Osama's genre on the same FBI's most wanted list in which Osama is now listed as deceased. At the rate of, say 1 trillion dollars each to kill them, it is a colossal amount. It begs the question: Is it worth it? Maybe addressing the underlying causes will be more cost effective. Besides others will keep replacing them, as has been the case so far.

---

[66] Al Jazeera TV English, news. 03 May, 2011

[67] Caroe, Olaf, *op. cit,*468, 477, *this story recalls an occasion, in February 1905 in Waziristan, when the Mahsud Companies in South Waziristan Militia had to be disbanded .It is revealing of the times and has the quality of tragedy.* Lt. Col Richard Harman was killed by a Mahsud recruit who was subsequently hanged by Sir Caroe, as a magistrate. He exuberantly dressed up and spent the last half hour in his cell blackening his eyelids with collyrium, to adorn himself for the maidens of Paradise. Appendix D, by E. B. Howell. *Armon* means grief, an adopted customary formula of lamentation. It is a Pashtu pronunciation of the Persian word *arman*.

Obvious reasons for this ongoing conflict, in order of urgency of their removal, are:

- US military presence in Saudi Arabia and elsewhere in the Middle East.
- Total and unquestioning endorsement of Israel's policy of genocide, apartheid and repression as practiced against the Palestinian people.
- Collusion with and abetment of corrupt and oppressive regimes in the region which suppress basic freedoms, loot and plunder.
- All the above to control Middle East oil.

One state of the art stealth helicopter crashed on site. It was blown up by the invading commandoes before departing the scene. Large pieces of it were collected by Pakistani authorities doing clean up and carted away for study and reverse engineering. All killings were in cold blood. There was no firefight and no weapons were found anywhere in the compound raided. As per usual practice, initially lies were put out by US authorities about a firefight and resistance on the part of those killed. These had to be quickly retracted when Pakistani authorities refused to accede go along. Those shot deliberately and wounded, included: one wife, a woman doctor and some children. Children watched the executions in real time. One twenty year old son of Osama was kidnapped for rendition and torture[68]. The press in USA was told that he escaped and went missing [sic], but nobody bought that. Pakistan military issued a vague warning about next time, which ostensibly

---

[68] The News International. 12 May, 2011, *ISI Officer Breaks the Ice on OBL Saga.* Islamabad, National news.

promised retaliation which may or may not materialize. Gruesome pictures of those killed were sold to Reuters and published worldwide.

Professor Mark Levine of UC Irvine and senior visiting researcher at the Centre for Middle Eastern Studies at Lund University in Sweden commented on Osama's death, *"The death of the al-Qaeda founder will, tragically wind up little more than a footnote in an ongoing set of wars that long ago lost their meaning and purpose[69]"*.

However, this son of Laden proved to a Godsend in case of Pakistan. He was the *cause célèbre* which brought all that US military and economic aid here, when he decided to live somewhere within the country. And in his death he exposed the severe shortcomings and inadequacies of the military and intelligence establishments of the country. The only two institutions which carried some hope for the future; all the other so called pillars of the state have long gone down the drain.

---

[69] Mark Levine, In Depth, Al Jazeera. net/English. 02 May, 2011

APPENDIX A

CIVIL DEFENCE MEASURE

Against Nuclear Biological, Chemical & conventional Attack

FIRST AID AND PRECAUTIONARY MEASURES AGAINST NUCLEAR, CHEMICAL, BIOLOGICAL AND CONVENTIONAL WEAPONS

Nuclear:

By taking following measures loss of life may be reduced to one third.

1. In view of the impending tragedy, leave congested places, big cities for mountainsides open places, bunkers/shelters/caves.
2. If in houses, keep windows open to escape effect of pressure wave blast.
3. Wear full clothing. Naked body parts are liable to get burnt by heat and radiation wave effect.
4. Do not keep combustible materials such as wood, petrol, diesel, cotton etc. in open. These are liable to catch fire.
5. After the explosion, stay calm, do not run out avoid stampeding.
6. After about 10 to 15 minutes, there will be atomic rainfall. Go into shelter to escape rainwater. It is radioactive.

7. Do not drink from open water utensil, channels, streams and ponds. Keep water covered. Otherwise it may be polluted by radioactivity.
8. Put multi layers or wet towel to cover your face.
9. Breathe through the filter mask or wet towel layers.
10. Drink excessive water and urinate frequently to release the inhaled or absorbed poisonous radioactive particulates.
11. East 2 to 3 Iodine tablets per day to lose absorbed radioactivity.
12. After half an hour of the explosion, leave your hiding place to go at least 10kilometer from the explosion site.

Chemical:

At the time of attack with chemical weapons, the following precautions are to be taken immediately and are to be continued upto atleast one/two hours after the attack.

1. Cover all parts of your body with heavy clothing, hands with gloves, feet with socks and shoes, mouth and nose with masks or wet towels, eyes with protective goggles, head and ears with a turban/cap/handkerchief/ear muffs etc.
2. Shelter in caves and bunkers etc. could be dangerous, avoid it. Shelters at higher places/mountains are preferred.
3. Move to a shelter from completely scaled to avoid ingress of gasses of the chemical weapon inside the shelter. An enter in the shelter may be through special filter made up of charcoal, filter paper, gas absorbing granules and wet cloth, curtain as in a

home air cooler. Move to open space one/two homes after the attack.

4. A pressurized room is a better choice so that no gases from outside enter the shelter room in case of chemical/nuclear attack.

5. Drink water in sufficient and urinate to dilute and remove the inhaled chemicals from the body.

6. Small oxygen cylinders or oxygen of liberating tablets should be available for use by those feeling suffocation.

7. Change clothes and have a shower after the attack to get rid of toxic chemicals/gases absorbed in the skin/clothes etc.

8. Decontamination of the area in common use of the inhabitant's soon after the attack by wet cloth, washing with water, baking soda or any other detergent.

Biological:

1. Fumigation in the vicinity of the inhabitants to avoid the ingress of biological agents.

2. Mask should be worn preferably having concentrated common salt.

3. Frequent bath using soap and detol could be helpful for protection against biological agents and washing of toxins etc.

Precautions against Anthrax Exposure:

1. Keep an air mask/towel in your hand to cover your ears eyes and nose.

2. Keep covered your face with multi layer cloth/filter mask if there is danger of attack.
3. Get vaccinated, if you have access to the vaccine and can afford it.
4. Have penicillin and doxyeyelline antibiotics at hand to start early treatment.
5. Keep your body clean, clothes clean wash frequently, gargle throat by saline water, wash eyes with saline water.

Protection against Fuel Air Bomb Attack:

The fuel air bomb drops a number of gas filled connister, which open at 100-200 meter altitude. Gases mix and cover an area as big as football ground. It is then remotely gritted. Burning of gases quickly consume oxygen and explosion produces, huge pressure wave which collapses lungs. Thus exposed person dies through suffocation.

Precautions:

1. Rush away from the site of explosion – if possible.
2. Cover your ears, eyes, and mouth by a strong mask with oxygen feed connection from the portable cylinder.
3. Door and window of the shelter places should be fully closed.
4. If in open lie down on the ground face downward, covered with layers of clothing.
5. Rush to the trenches, caves, and be down with layers of clothing.

6. Keep lying in your shelter for few minutes after the explosion. Breath heavily again and again.
7. Victims should be helped by oxygen and helped to breathe.
8. If oxygen not available, help the victim to breath by repeated processing and releasing chest.
9. Be careful that enemy attack again soon after, therefore does not leave your safety places.
10. In case there is ground fire take normal precaution, move away, escape yourself from smoke and heat; try to put off flare by sand, water and beating according to the normal firefighting practices.

Civil Defence Measures Against Nuclear Weapon Attack:

Atomic bomb attack is devastating in nature. Extent of damage coned, however, he considerably less if preparedness against this terrible situation has been done carefully.

We cannot adopt steps that USA, USSR and China have adopted because those are too costly. We in Pakistan have our own strategy. Avoiding exorbitant expenditure, we can take the following steps:-

1. Define which Government institutions should adopt what safety measures before and after the nuclear attack.
2. Develop and implement measures for preparedness against nuclear attack through concerted efforts of

specialists and chief executives of all related civil and military formations.

3. Study Nuclear Defence System for Pakistan.
4. Form district level sub-committees for implementing the recommended measures.
5. Create trained nuclear defence rescue teams with necessary equipment in each unit.
6. Spell out line of authority at every level to handle emergencies without having to wait for advice from higher level after the catastrophe.
7. Strengthen civil defence department in all provinces with nuclear experts/scientists to assist on supervising and implementing the safety measures and also impart training to the public in regard in regard to this role they are to play in case of a nuclear attack.
8. Create awareness among the public through delivering specially prepared lectures about what to do in such on eventuality.
9. Teach children in high schools and colleges about the basics of defence and radioactivity decontamination measures after a nuclear weapons attack.
10. Educate the public about the extent of damage that can be caused by exposure to nuclear radiation and about the necessary precautions against radioactive fall out, and about handling of the contaminated items.

CIVIL PREPAREDNESS AGAINST NUCLEAR ATTACK
Sultan Bashir-Ud-Din Mahmood

Introduction:

In the present scenario of the world when many countries of the world have got nuclear weapons, danger of nuclear war cannot be ruled out. Consequently, entire scenario of Civil and Military Defence has changed now. Therefore it is imperative on civil defence authorities to seriously think over and preempt measures about preparedness against nuclear attacks, and to incorporate them in their agenda of national defence as everyone is concerned about the qurtia: "Is there any defence against Nuclear Weapons attack?" and "What can they contribute to minimize the after effects of the attack?" Yes, there is defence against Nuclear Weapons also. Firstly, it is to destroy the incoming delivery vehicle before it crosses your border. If bomb's triggering device has not been activated, possibility of a nuclear explosion in that case is extremely remote. Even if the enemy does trigger the bomb in panic, it will be off its target, or explode at high altitudes, thus extent of damage will be relatively less, depending upon where and at what altitude the bomb exploded. However, in this paper we are mainly concerned about the civil "Preparedness Against Nuclear Attack", that is what measures the Government and the people can take to control and minimize the destructive effects of the tragedy.

Nature of Damage:

Needless to say that effect of nuclear weapon attack on any city can be disastrous as is evident from the halo cast of Hiroshima and Nagasaki in August 1945. Those nuclear weapons were equivalent to 12 Kilo Ton and 23 Kilo Ton of TNT respectively, but sudden loss of property and life was unheard of in the human history. In Hiroshima, out of the total population of 256300 people, 68000 died and additional 76000 suffered severe injuries in the first hour of the explosion.

In any nuclear explosion damage is mainly due to blast wave energy, thermal exposure, and initial nuclear radiation. Close to two-thirds of those died at Hiroshima during the first day after explosion were reported to have been badly burned. High incidence of flesh burns caused by thermal radiation among both fatalities and survivors in Japan was undoubtedly related to the light and scanty clothing worn, because of warm weather prevailing at the time of attack. Quite a large percentage of those who wore sufficient clothes or were in houses, schools, or offices, survived due to shielding provided against flesh thermal radiation.

After initial damage, the subsequent damage was caused due to fires from inflammable materials such as petroleum, gas, and other combustible materials, and that from the falling debris of buildings due to earth tremors and high-speed windstorm blowing towards the epicenter.

Another cause of loss of life was due to stampeding by the panic-stricken citizens rushing out of city facing blockage of roads and escape routes. If there had been proper preparedness number of deaths due to such secondary causes could have been much less. As regards loss of life due to radiations, it might be very high in the 2-3 Kilometer radius of the explosion center. Beyond that short term loss is generally expected to below but long-term health hazards are likely to continue several years. With a 20 Kilo Ton Atomic bomb (same as Hiroshima) the explosion site may experience crater of about 300 to 500 meter radius, 15 to 25 meter depths at the epicenter of explosion, and debris spread over further 200 to 300 meters. Very little may survive in about one kilometer radius around the epicenter. Most of the civil structures except steel and strong concrete buildings may be wiped out. But beyond 2 Kilometer radius, possibility of surviving are quite good. Particularly those shielded in buildings or underground shelters, have very good chances. Beyond two Kilometers from the center of explosion, extent of the damage will gradually diminish and many building may remain standing. Buildings are liable to be damaged due to secondary causes; due to winds blowing at speed of several hundred kilometers from the outside toward the explosion site. This may lift weak, fallen brick masonry structures. Then there will be fires, which may break out in the explosion area. Overall loss would depend upon many factors such as power of the device, altitude of explosion, environment conditions at the time of explosion of secondary fires, escape routes etc. However good preparedness measures, can help to reduce loss to less than one half of what could occur without that. Thus preparedness against Nuclear weapon attack is of vital national importance to protect life, property and morale of the people as also in regard to control of the situation by the civil and military authorities.

Need of Preparedness:

Many of these measures are akin to common civil defense practice. For example, if population is educated and trained to face such an eventuality and if escape routes are thorough, not congested and if the chances of secondary fires have been curtailed by proper layout and the damage due to falling of buildings is taken care of, catastrophic impact of a nuclear attack could be manageable.

People who have taken refuge in their houses will be relatively safe against heat burns. Those who escaped in shelters such as deep underground bunkers, subways, basements etc. would be safer than those who would take refuge in the over ground buildings. Beyond one kilometer, underground shelters with 3 to 5 meters over burden may remain intact and people under them will mostly survive. Caves, mountain shelters and strong bunkers will provide good shelters to the occupants.

Buildings with wide openings and windows will have greater chances to remain standing as compared to close door buildings. Similarly, high rising buildings will collapse much more than the low standing buildings.

Worst hit will be the masonry structures; very few of them may hold themselves even at a distance of 5 Km from the epicenter. However, high ductility building such as well designed reinforced concrete buildings and steel structures are mostly likely to remain standing beyond 2 Km radius from the epicenter and thus shall provide good degree of safety to their inmates.

To reduce and control the secondary climates, proper escape routes are also of great importance. In case these are not sufficiently wide and well defined, a very large number of people may be caught in the fires, falling debris, or may die by stampeding.

Following are the recommended measures to control ill effects and to reduce the loss of life after an atomic attack.

A: Institutional Measures:

1. Government institutions be defined and assigned responsibility for safety measures before and after the nuclear attack.
2. For this purpose, an inter ministerial level national committee including representatives of armed forces, Provincial Chief Ministers, and civil defence bodies may be instituted with the responsibility for central coordination functions to develop and implement measures for "Preparedness Against Nuclear Attack on Pakistan".
3. The national committee may form sub committees at the city levels to implement the recommended measures.
4. Every strategic organization may have a trained nuclear defence unit and rescue teams equipped with equipment necessary for this purpose.
5. Line of authority be clearly spelled out at every level to handle emergencies without the need of interaction from higher level after the catastrophe. All civil hospitals should be trained to handle with due care radiation injuries cases.

B: Educational Measures:

1. Public should be educated about the "Preparedness Against Nuclear Attack" through especially prepared lectures programs on television, radio and in newspapers by experts in order to create awareness about what to do in such an eventuality.
2. Armed personnel and college students should be taught about the basics of defence against atomic weapons; and trained radioactivity decontamination measures.
3. Public be educated by lectures, radio talks etc about the extent of damage which can be caused by exposure to nuclear radiations and the necessary precautions against radioactive fall out, and handling of the contaminated items, which they should take to escape the damage.

C: General Measures:

1. Very important offices and command centers, be shifted away from the cities in the underground buildings or deep caves in mountains fitted with emergency controls. Over burden should not be less than five meter.
2. All big cities, should have adequately designed underground shelters such as subways in different areas of the city, fitted with the radioactive air cleaning devices; and civil facilities enough to last for at least one week.
3. Hospitals should be provided with kits to treat the cases of radiation burns and exposures.

4. Doctors should be educated to treat and handle the cases of radiation burns, and exposure to high radioactivity burn units in the hospitals should be strengthened to cater for sudden large-scale emergency.
5. The WIP communication links be constructed underground and proper redundancy may be provided on such routes.
6. Power lines in two important places/offices should be laid down underground to reduce chances of fire and electrocuting in the event of emergency.
7. Very important civil and military centers should be provided independent diesel generators/charged battery to supplement the normal electric power supply.

D: Every Person Measures:

1. Building windows should be kept open.
2. People should stay inside their houses, preferably in underground shelters or in mountain caves.
3. Men, women and children should be fully dressed.
4. If you can, leave the congested places, go to open area, preferably villages; or mountainsides.
5. Every house/office should have sufficient quantity of water stored in drums or buckets, which must be properly covered.
6. Do not stay near the site of explosion within ten kilometers radius. Wash your clothing body parts thoroughly, if you were within six kilometer of the explosion site.
7. Drink water in as much quantity as possible and urinate frequently. Eat good food, remain calm and

take part in rescue measures keeping your trust in ALLAH.

US AIR CAMPAIGN IN AFGHANISTAN

Introduction:

The typical targets for any air force in wartime are radar installations, air bases, command and control buildings, telecommunication infrastructure, storage areas, railway lines, roads, bridges, etc. in Afghanistan, the above infrastructure is virtually nonexistent. Hence, the motives of US air campaign in Afghanistan are fundamentally different. Under the garb of fighting terrorism US will be targeting human beings in this air campaign. In this antihuman campaign their primary weapons will be antipersonnel bombs rather than anti-radiation missile, anti-runway bombs, or other smart weapons designed to destroy tanks missile batteries or the targets listed above. The terrain of Afghanistan, which can act as a natural cover reconnaissance effort will be required to localize and track the movement of Taliban forces in the absence of heavy equipment.

Reconnaissance:

The air campaign will commence with reconnaissance missions. The success of aerial strikes will largely depend upon the accuracy of information collected in the reconnaissance flights. By blocking or impeding the reconnaissance effort, Taliban may succeed in delaying the aerial strikes. The objectives of reconnaissance fights may include:

- Detection, and localization of Taliban forces
- Identification of their command and control centers
- Identification of storage areas and supply lines

- Terrain mapping for launch of cruise missiles and familiarization of US Pilots

A number of aerial vehicles will be available to US for reconnaissance purposes. Some of these are discussed below:

1. Specialized High altitude aircraft. These include U-2 or SR-71 type aircraft, which have been used for spying against the Soviet Union. Since they operate from a very high altitude, they can only pick up large high value targets. In a guerrilla war they will be of little utility. Hence, Taliban should not be concerned about them. Moreover, there is nothing Taliban can do about them.

2. The second kind of platform will be F-15, F-16, F-18, or other fighter aircraft equipped with reconnaissance equipment. This equipment is likely to include, visual cameras, thermal imagers or FLIR, laser range finders, and elintsigint equipment. The Americans are unlikely to use them unless they are sure that Taliban do not possess any means to shoot them down. For detailed information they will have to fly at low altitudes and may be vulnerable to stinger type heat seeking missiles. However, Americans may use them for terrain mapping from a high altitude.

3. The main workhorse of US reconnaissance effort will be unmanned aerial vehicles (UAVs). Since they are unmanned they can fly at low altitudes and low speeds to capture a microscopic view. Low speed and low altitude will also make them easiest target. Once they are detected AAA may be adequate to

shoot them down. Please note that Stinger will not be effective against UAVs as they do not emit any infrared radiation in the 3-5 micron band. Stinger and other heat seeking missiles track radiation in this band. Detection of UAVs may be the most difficult part as they are small and relatively silent. Nevertheless, they can be visually observed from a distance of 1- 2 KMs, which is also the range in which AAA is effective. Thermal imagers which typically operate in 8-14 micron infrared band can also pick them during night as well as day time from similar distances. Finally, they do have some noise that can be heard once they are very close.

4. Helicopters are also ideal for reconnaissance in guerrilla war as they can hover over a small area for long periods and come down to low altitudes very conveniently. Helicopters are easy to pick up from their noise. Their visual observability is also quite high. Moreover, they will be carrying a crew, which makes them a high-risk platform for the Americans. Nevertheless, they will be inclined to use it against Taliban. AAA could be quite effective against helicopters should it be available in close proximity.

5. Another reconnaissance vehicle is a much smaller version of UAVs called miniature aerial vehicle (MAV). MAVs are smaller than one meter and usually hand launched. They do not possess a long range and are primarily used by ground troops. They are difficult to spot and shoot because of their small size low noise. Northern Alliance could also be equipped with this kind of aid. The best counter against MAVs may be jamming of its communication link. In case Taliban do not possess this capability

Taliban may not worry about it as it may not be very potent in a hilly terrain where it will have to fly at higher altitudes.

A.   Anti-Personnel Weapons:

As discussed earlier the American air campaign will largely utilize anti-personnel weapons. Surgical precision will be quite irrelevant; instead a large footprint will be important criteria. Hence, smart or guided weapons will not play a significant role in this campaign. Subsequent paragraphs describe some of the ant-personnel weapons available to US.

1.   Fuel air explosive (FAE) is perhaps the most inhuman and lethal weapon in the American arsenal. It has been extensively used in Operation Desert Strom against Al Qaeda troops. It is designed to kill human beings by a pressure wave followed by a vacuum in which no oxygen is available. The sequence of operation is as follows: a) the bomb is released from a high altitude; b) The shell of the bomb splits open and three canisters containing the fuel are released at a predetermined height; c) the canisters open and spread the fuel in the air; d) once the optimum stoichiometric ratio is attained in the atmosphere after a specified time the fuel is ignited by a fuse; e) ignition of the explosive mixture of gases creates a pressure wave of several bars that crushes the organs of human beings. The pressure wave is followed by a vacuum in the same region. The FAE may be countered by premature ignition of the fuel. This may be accomplished by targeting the FAE bomb as soon as it is released with AAA loaded

with a mix of tracer and normal bullets. Since the bombs descend under gravity the FAE will take tens of seconds to complete the sequence described above. The descent of canisters may be further retarded by parachutes; in which case they will be small but slow targets for AAA. The purpose of AAA will be to firstly knock out the bomb or canisters before they release the explosive gases and secondly premature ignition of the fuel.

2. The second type of antipersonnel bomb may be the pre-fragmented bomb. A conventional steel bomb, or unitary warhead is meant to destroy concrete or steel structures. Hence, the steel fragments that fly out after the explosions are quite large and few in numbers. Also, they do not travel over long distances. The pre-fragmented bomb, on the other hand, is filled with approximately 40,000 steel balls of less than 1 cm diameter. No energy is wasted in fragmenting the steel structure and the steel balls fly out to long distances. Unlike the steel bomb the pre-fragmented bomb is exploded at an altitude of 8-10 meters to maximize the effective radius or footprint. The footprint of a pre fragmented bomb maybe 4-5 times larger than that of steel bomb. The best protection against the pre-fragmented bombs may be the natural cover available in the hilly terrain of Afghanistan. Pre fragmented bombs will be a very difficult target for AAA. They can be dropped from a low altitude and do not have long sequence of operation like the FAE. Caves may be the best protection against pre-fragmented bombs but they are highly vulnerable to FAE. Hence, the Americans may drop these two types of bombs simultaneously.

3. The third type of antipersonnel bomb may be the programmed sub munitions dispenser or the cluster bomb. The cluster bomb dispenses about 150 - 200 bomb lets or land mines about the size of a hand grenade in a given area. The outer shell of the cluster bomb is physically similar to FAE and opens in mid air releasing the bomb lets. The bomb lets do not explode upon landing on ground. Instead, they will explode in a preprogrammed sequence in the next 24 hours. They may explode once disturbed by handling. Cluster bomb is an area denial weapon meant to keep enemy troops out of the footprint of the weapon while friendly forces who know the detonation sequence can operate in the territory when the bomb lets are not exploding. US may use this weapon in support of the Northern alliance. Since the bomb lets are about the size of a hand grenade, Taliban infantry can visually spot them and avoid them or perhaps destroy them by firing shots at them. Cluster bomb is not the most serious threat to Taliban.

B. Conclusion:

In conclusion the US air campaign in Afghanistan will be an antipersonnel campaign i.e. the targets will be human beings in hilly terrain. Reconnaissance activity will be vital for the success of this campaign. The first layer of defense for Taliban should be blocking or hindering the reconnaissance effort by shooting down the UAVs with AAA. The second layer of defense will be use of Stinger against low flying aircraft. The most potent weapon that these aircraft will deliver is the FAE. The best strategy against FAE may be premature ignition with the help of AAA loaded with tracer bullets. Taliban need not worry about the cluster bomb or the pre-fragmented bomb as much but they must work out a strategy to counter the effect of FAE.

CHEMICAL WARFARE

Chemical warfare (CW) is the direct military use of chemicals to injure or kill humans, or plants. Although the chemicals are commonly referred to as "poison gases," they can be in any physical state---gas, liquid, or solid.

CW Agents:

CW chemicals are known as CW agents and are often categorized according to their effect. Because oftentimes their proper chemical names are hard to use, agents are frequently referred to by the codes of symbols. Table 1 lists eight CW agent categories and gives examples of each with the symbols used by many western nations, including the United States and United Kingdom.

Table 1. Chemicals Used by the Military as CW Agents

Agent Category	Common Military Name (Military Code)
Nerve	Tabun (GA), Sarin (GB), Soman (GD), VX, VR-55
Blister	Distilled mustard or yperite (HD), Lewisite (L), Mustard / Lewisite mixture (HL), nitrogen mustard (HN), phosgene oxime (CX)
Blood	Hydrogen cyanide (AC), cyanogen chloride (CK), arsine (SA)
Choking	Phosgene (CG), diphosgene (DP), chlorine
Incapacitating	BZ
Vomiting	Adamsite (DM)
Tear	CN,CS
Herbicide	Agent blue, Agent Orange

Nerve Agents:

Nerve agents keep the nervous system from functioning properly by inhibiting enzymes responsible for destroying acetylcholine, a body chemical vital to nerve signal transmission. This behavior is referred to as cholinesterase inhibition. This behavior is referred to as cholinesterase inhibition. Nerve agents cause acetylcholine to accumulate at nerve ending, and normal function becomes impossible.

The nerve agents are organophosphorus chemicals, or organophosphates. The Germans recognized the potential military value of organophosphates in 1934 and, by the end of the Second World War, had synthesized three nerve agents deemed suitable for combat use. These compounds were named Tabun, Sarin, and Soman. The compounds were given the code designations GA, GB, and GD, respectively.

By 1958 the Americans had selected an organophosphate known simply as VX. Soviet research produced VR-55, a compound similar to VX.

Symptoms:

Early symptoms of nerve agent's exposure include runny nose, drooling, pinpointing of the pupils (miosis), and muscle spasms. If untreated, nerve agent poisoning leads to paralysis, with death by suffocation.

Treatment:

Atropine is the classical treatment to counteract nerve agents. It provides some protection against the excess acetylcholine that accumulates. In addition, chemicals called oximes that reverse cholinesterase inhibition are an effective antidote against some but not all nerve agents.

Blister Agents:

Blister agents, or vesicants, cause wounds resembling those caused by burns. The first blister agent was distilled mustard (HD), named for its mustard-like odor. Although commonly called mustard gas, HD is normally a liquid or aerosol when dispersed in combat. Other blister agents include the nitrogen mustard (HN), lewiste (L), and phosgene oxime (CX).

Blistering and other burn-like injuries are common to all blister agents.
Exposure to L and CX causes immediate and intense pain as well. A mixture of distilled mustard and lewisite (known as HL) extends the useful temperature range for HD, remaining liquid at temperatures where HD alone would freeze. Blister agents can be lethal, causing dry land drowning where the lungs fill up with fluids. Military interest in blister agents was sparked by their ability to disrupt routine combat operations.

Protection:

Depending upon the weather these agents routinely persist for hours to weeks, and some reports document persistence on the order of months and years. Such persistence demands extended wear of personal protective equipment, such as gloves, masks, boots, and clothing.

Blood Agents:

Blood agents inhibit proper use of oxygen by the body. They disrupt cellular energy production, and the resultant lack of oxygen causes. If that condition persists all life processes come to an end.

Blood agents are among the fastest acting of all poisons. Examples include Hydrogen cyanide (AC) and arsine (SA).

Choking Agents:

Choking agents primarily injure the eyes and the respiratory track (nose, throat, and lungs). They cause the tissues to swell, making breathing difficult and leading to dry land drowning. Chlorine and phosgene (CG) are choking agents as well as valued commercial chemicals. Both were used in the first CW attacks during the First World War and initial use was extensive. However, difficulties in controlling their release made them impractical as CW agents, and they came to be replaced by other chemicals, especially the blister agents.

Incapacitating Agents:

Incapacitating agents are intended to make an enemy cease fighting without injury or death. They are intended to produce physiological or mental effects that render victims incapable of carrying out their military duties. As yet, no truly effective incapacitating agent has been found.

Vomiting Agents:

These agents typically arsenic-containing compounds include extreme nausea leading to uncontrollable vomiting. The British used vomiting agents in North Russia against the Red Army in 1919.

Of low to moderate toxicity, vomiting agents were of significant interest for the possible use in law-enforcement activities or riot control and saw some limited use for such purposes in the 1930s. By the agreement, the western nations banned the use of vomiting agents against civilians. There is no record of their combat use after 1920.

Tear Agents:

Tear agents, or lachrymators, cause copious tear flow and irritate the skin. Because their effects are rapid but transitory, these agents are widely used for training, riot control, and other situations were long term incapacitation is unacceptable. They can cause serious injury or death if used in confined spaces.

Herbicides:

Herbicides destroy vegetation and are important commercially for such applications as weed control. They have been considered for military use to destroy or limit crop production and to remove leaves from plants (defoliation). Some crop destruction by deliberate military use of herbicides occurred during the Vietnam War when the Americans used Agent Blue, an arsenic-containing chemical, to prevent grain formation in rice fields.

During this same period, the Americans also experiment with a variety of defoliants. They selected Agent Orange, which was employed to defoliate entire forests, thus denying their use by the enemy for cover and concealment.

Related Developments:

Since the mid - 1960s, research has concentrated on ways to make existing agents more effective.
1.   The first of the means for enhancing effectiveness is to add a polymer. The thickened agent is more difficult to remove and takes longer to evaporate; both these attribute increase the CW hazard.
2.   Another development is the use of a binary system, which uses two chemicals that mix on contact to form a CW agent. In its ideal form, a binary system would have two chemicals of low toxicity that react

completely to form a highly poisonous substance. A binary system has the advantage of less difficulty in storage, transportation, and handling.

3. A third mean of enhancing CW agent performance is that of incorporating a chemical that degrades the protective measures used against CW attack. For instance, a chemical that quickly overcomes the protective ingredients in a gas mask filter might be mixed with a CW agent. The first chemical, called a mask penetrator or defeater, would destroy the filter, allowing the CW agent to get through and harm the individual wearing that mask.

Effectiveness of Chemical Weapons:

For various reasons, effective combat use of CW agents is difficult to predict. Wind speed and direction control CW agent spread upon release and a shift in wind can bring the agent back upon attacking force. Other weather conditions, such as sunlight, temperature and precipitation influence how long the CW contamination will persist. Topography and type terrain influences CW agents spread and persistence once the target is hit. The level of preparedness of the intended target determines its ability to withstand and attack. For these reasons and others, military planners are not inclined to call for the use of CW agents. Traditionally, CW agents were selected for their toxicity, with preference given to agents of the highest lethality. Recent examination of CW, however, has noted its ability to bog down military operations and thus change the pace of battle. This change comes about in part because of required CW defensive measures. Such measures as burdensome individual protective gear, fully enclosed protective shelters, and labor-intensive means for detecting and neutralizing contamination are invoked by prudent commanders for operations in both a known CW environment and a suspected one.

ANTHRAX - A LETHAL BIOLOGICAL WEAPON

Biological Warfare:

Biological warfare can be considered the military use of living organisms or associated materials that are intended to cause disability, disease, or death in humans, animals, or crops for hostile purposes. Agents include pathogenic microorganisms; toxins and bioactive substances, which may be weaponised, using both military and civilian type delivery systems.

After World War-11 the development of biological weapons assumed a relatively low priority in the arms race. But recent advances in biotechnology have made possible the more efficient production of increasingly destructive viruses and bacteria. Their use is not currently controlled by international verification procedures such as those that apply for example, to nuclear arms so they are relatively cheaper to produce, hide and launch.

The commonest biological warfare items are Anthrax and Botulinum.

Common Agents of Biological Warfare:

- Bacillus Anthracis (anthrax)
- Clostridium Botulinum (botulism)
- Yersinia pestis (plague)
- Varsaela major(small pox)
- Francisella tularensis (tularemia)
- Viral hemmorrhagic fever

171

- Brucella species (brucellosis)
- Staphylococcus enterotoxin B

Common Chemical Agents of Warfare:

- Distilled Mustard
- Lewisite
- Mustard gas
- Nitrogen Mustard
- Phosgene oxime
- Sarine
- Cynogen chloride
- Hydrogen chloride
- Hydrogen cyanide
- Chlorine
- Nitrogen oxide
- Phosuene
- Sulfur trioxide-chlorosulfonic Acid
- Titanium tetrachloride.

Anthrax:

Anthrax is an acute infectious disease caused by the spore forming bacterium Bacillus Anthracis. It is one of the most serious and dangerous of all organisms that could be used as a biological weapon. Anthrax most commonly Occurs in wild and domestic vertebrates (cattle, sheep, goats, camels, antelopes, and other herbivores), but it can also occur in humans when they are exposed to infected animals or tissue from infected animals or through a weapon.

Anthrax - a current issue:

Anthrax is considered to be a potential agent for use in biological warfare, due its lethal effects, early un detect ability and easy production. It is a fear for the western world, as many terrorists out fits are believed to posses' anthrax. However its use by major powers of the world during recent wars has also been reported over civilians and military personnel. In the present world scenario it is important that all people should know something about anthrax. It has been claimed that all the American troops (Army, Navy, and Air force) plus every person in the reserve force has already been vaccinated against Anthrax. There are also reports that the whole population of Israel including the forces and the public has been compulsorily vaccinated against Anthrax.

Global Prevalence of Anthrax:

Anthrax is found globally. It is more common in developing countries or countries without veterinary public health programs and lack of vaccination facilities against Anthrax. Certain regions of the world report more Anthrax in animals than others. B. Anthracis spores can live in the soil for many years, and humans can become infected with Anthrax by handling products from infected animals or by inhaling anthrax spores from contaminated animal products. Eating undercooked meat from infected animals can also spread Anthrax.

Since late 70's Anthrax has been reported to be cultured and developed for potential use in terrorist and mass killing activities. The weapons that have been developed include aerosolized `Anthrax Bombs' that can be lodged through missiles or aircrafts; and `Anthrax Sprays' that can be used through any aerosol device like a cologne bottle or for bigger area by Helicopter crop duster machines. It is reported that more than 70 countries of the world and numerous terrorist organizations posses such weapons.

Microbiology of B. Anthracis:

B. Anthracis is an aerobic, gram positive, spore forming, nonmotile Bacillus specie. The non-flagellated vegetative cell is large. Spore size is approximately 1-micro meter. Anthrax spores germinate when they enter an environment rich in amino acids, nucleosides, and glucose, such as that found in the blood or tissues of animals or humans.

Mode of Transmission & Symptoms:

Natural Anthrax disease is most common in agricultural regions where it occurs in animals. When Anthrax affects humans, it is usually due to an occupational exposure to infected animals or their products. Butchers and other animal handlers are also susceptible as they some time may come across an infected animal.

But the future holds new avenues for mass scale deaths due to Anthrax (inhalational anthrax) as a result of it's biological warfare potential.

Anthrax infection can occur in three forms:

- Cutaneous
- Inhalational

- Gastrointestinal.

CUTANEOUS: Most (95%) anthrax infection occur when the bacterium enters a cut or an abrasion on the Skin. Such as when handling contaminated wool, hides, leather or hair products (especially goat hair) of infected animals. Skin infection begins as a raised itchy bump that resembles an insect bite but within I-2 days develops into vesicle and then a painless ulcer, usually 1-3 cm in diameter, with a characteristic black necrotic (dying) area in the centre. Lymph glands in the adjacent area may swell. About 20% of untreated cases of cutaneous anthrax will result in death, which is rare with appropriate antimicrobial therapy.

INHALATIONAL: It is almost always due to inhalation of B. anthracis spores and is usually a consequence of biological warfare. Initial symptoms may resemble a common cold/flu. After 48-96 hrs (40% cases) and after 5-10 days (60% cases) the symptoms may progress to severe breathing prOsama Bin Ladenems and shock. Inhalation Anthrax is usually fatal. The patient is found to have hemorrhagic thoracic lymphadenitis and hemmorhagic mediastinitis and sometimes meningitis. Chest X-ray shows mediastinlal widening but clear lung fields. Sudden fever, dyspnea, diaphoresis, stridor and finally shock are other common Symptoms.

GASTROINTESTINAL: The intestinal disease form of Anthrax may follow the consumption of contaminated meat and is characterized by an acute inflammation of the intestinal tract. It occurs in orophatyngeal and abdominal forms. Initial signs of nausea, loss of appetite, vomiting, fever, are followed by abdominal pain, vomiting of blood, and severe diarrhea. Intestinal Anthrax results in death in 25% to 60 % of cases.

Diagnosis of Anthrax:

Anthrax is diagnosed by isolating B. anthracis from the blood, skin lesions, or respiratory secretions or by measuring specific antibodies in the blood of persons with suspected cases. Such facilities are not available in the 3rd world. So here diagnosis only depends on early clinical diagnosis by trained doctors and paramedical staff.

Spread of Anthrax:

A 50 kg. Bomb thrown in the centre of a city with 5 million people can affect over half of the population. Spread is dependent on air movement, wind velocity and weather. Most people get exposed in the first 24 hours. Direct person-to-person spread of Anthrax is extremely unlikely to occur. Communicability is not a concern in managing or visiting patients with inhalation Anthrax.

If there are any previous cuts or abrasions on the skin deposition of the organism leading to cutaneous anthrax is 11 possibilities.

Prevention:

VACCINE: A vaccine has been developed for anthrax and is reported to be 93% effective in protecting humans against anthrax. Besides being costly this vaccine is not freely available. Only one institute in USA has been licensed to manufacture it and its sale is restricted to military use only. There is also evidence that Israel has got a vaccine plant (probably larger than the American) but it has not been confirmed. Russia has got one plant for manufacturing Anthrax vaccine for animals (this is not safe for human use) and there vaccine is available in the market.

MASK: Use of plastic masks with cotton and polypropylene packed inside can be helpful in reducing the risk of inhaling- the spores. These masks (although expensive) are available in the western markets. For poor countries the only option remains is of cotton masks. Even wet towel to cover the face can also be helpful. But the basic problem is this that Anthrax is colorless and odorless. There is no way that one can know that Anthrax spores are present around him! So how can one use a mask? However it is recommended that on getting any news of such outbreak or attack one should wear the mask at all times.

TREATMENT: If treatment is initiated early after exposure this can reduce mortality by half: but again this requires diagnosis and such facilities are not available readily in the developing countries.

The Anthrax Vaccine:

The Anthrax vaccine is a cell-free filtrate vaccine, which means it contains no dead or live bacteria in the preparation The final product contains no more than 2.4 mg of aluminum hydroxide as adjutant. Anthrax vaccines intended for animals should not be used in humans.

Following Groups should be vaccinated:

- Persons who work directly with the organism in the laboratory

- Persons who work with imported animal's hides or furs in areas where standards are insufficient to prevent exposure to anthrax spores.
- Persons who handle potentially infected animal products in high-incidence areas.
- Military personnel deployed to areas with high risk for exposure to the organism (as when it is used as a biological warfare weapon).
- Pregnant women should be vaccinated if only it is absolutely necessary.
- And people who are at a recognized threat of a biological weapon.

The immunization consists of three subcutaneous injections given 2 weeks apart followed by three additional subcutaneous injections given at 6. 12. and 18 months. Annual booster injections of the vaccine are recommended thereafter.

Mild local reactions occur in 30 % of the recipients of the vaccine and consist of slight tenderness and redness at the site of the injection. Severe local reactions are infrequent and consist of extensive swelling of the forearm in addition to the local reaction. Systemic reactions occur in less than 0.2 % of the recipients.

Treatment for Anthrax:

Doctors can prescribe effective antibiotics. To be effective, treatment should be initiated early. If left untreated; the disease can be fatal. Most naturally occurring anthrax strains are sensitive to Penicillin and Doxycycline. It is suggested that antibiotic therapy be continued for 60 days, with oral therapy replacing intravenous therapy as soon as the condition of the patient improves. Other antibiotics effective against B. anthracis in vitro include chloramphenicol, erythromycin, macrolides, aminoglycosides, cefazolin, and other first generation cephalosporins.

Decontaminated of Area after Anthrax Attack:

In case of intentional aerosolization of Anthrax spores, decontamination is based on

- Evidence concerning aerosolization
- Anthrax spore survival
- Environmental exposure

The greatest risk to human health following an intentional aerosolization of anthrax spores occurs during the period in which anthrax spores remain airborne, called as primary aerosolization. The duration for which spores remain airborne and the distance spores travel before they become noninfectious or fall to the ground is dependent on the weather conditions and aerobiological properties of the dispersed aerosol.

Secondary aerosolization is the process of re suspension of spores from the ground or other surface later due to strong wind. It is an unlikely occurrence.

If an environmental surface is proved to be heavily contaminated with anthrax spores in the immediate area of spill or close proximity to the point of release of an anthrax aerosol, decontamination of that area may decrease the slight risk of acquiring anthrax by secondary aerosolization. However, decontamination of large urban areas or even a building following an exposure to an anthrax aerosol would be extremely difficult and is not indicated. Although tile risk of disease caused by secondary acrosolization would be extremely low, it would be difficult to offer absolute assurance that there was no risk whatsoever.

Post-exposure vaccination, if vaccine is available, can be a possible intervention that could further lower the risk of anthrax infection in this setting.

In the setting of announced alleged anthrax release, every person coming in direct contact with the alleged substance should receive post exposure antibiotic coverage until the substance is proved not to be anthrax. If the alleged substance is proved to be anthrax, immediate consultation with experts should be obtained.

All dead bodies (of animals and humans) should be cremated/disposed of properly. Graves should be deep so that animals cannot reach them. As if an animal eats a corpse infected with anthrax it will also develop the disease and if in turn a human eats that animal the disease will further spread.

Conclusion:

Anthrax is dangerous and is a real threat to all of us in this world. Whenever a biological attack will happen probably none of us both in the developed and the undeveloped world will know what we are inhaling until most of us have been affected. The best course to protect ourselves will be:

1. To get vaccinated, if you have 'access' to the vaccine and can afford it.
2. To raise a voice against use of such weapons as civilians are the biggest casualties.
3. To keep an air mask/towels in your hand bag all the time!
4. To have penicillin and Doxycycline at hand to start early treatment.
5. And to pray to God that nobody is so cruel to use it on innocent people who have no enmity with anybody except a desire to live their lives the way they like.

APPENDIX B

The President of Pakistan,
Islamic Republic of Pakistan,
Islamabad
Your Excellency,

Date: August 6, 2007

It is submitted that I, Humayun Niaz, NIC No. 61101-7788430-1, was mentally tortured and financially ruined, due to my incarceration by the Govt. of Pakistan (Intelligence Bureau), on the bidding of U. S Intelligence Agencies for a period of 33 days; from 11 Nov. to 14 Dec. 2001. This detention was for interrogation/ investigation to ascertain the whereabouts of the elite Taliban after 9/11. I did not have the faintest idea of what was being asked. The questions were ridiculous and seemed like a farce to me. I remember thinking at that time that these people are doing all this to please their high-ups and to show some action, any action.

I am a retired Naval Officer and familiar with intelligence work through various professional courses/ assignments during service. I regret to say that the whole episode was not handled professionally from the outset. All that was required was a phone call or a visit by the assigned officer, and all their doubts would have cleared in a day. As they indeed did after 33 days. What was the point in kidnapping me while I was going for (Isha) prayers on that day? What were they trying to prove and to whom? It does not make sense to use a sledgehammer to kill a fly.

The background to this kidnapping was a flourmill established by me (with contributions from friends), in Kandahar, Afghanistan from Dec. 2000 to Sept. 2001. The mill is still standing, and a U.S FBI officer told me, during a session that had there been any doubts in their (Americans') minds about the veracity of this mill it would have been razed to the ground. This project was established at great peril and hardship at that time but generated a lot of goodwill and understanding between 2 brotherly countries. The undertaking was, and still is in the National Interest of Pakistan.

Losses suffered by the project due to my incarceration are as follows:

S.No	Item	Amount
1	Due to loss of contract for purchase of wheat from Torghundi	Rs. 1.5 Crore (110 thousand £ approx)
2	Non-installation of diesel generator, (subsequently lost)	1 Crore
3	Late fees/ fines imposed by Afghan Govt.	15 Lakh (10 thousand £)
4	Delay in ongoing works till completion	20 Lakh
5	Depreciation/ inflation losses	50 Lakh
	Total	**3, 35, 00,000**

I have not been able to make up this loss, in spite of relentless efforts over the last 6 years. Most of the funds generated for the mill were the life savings of retirees like me. It is requested that this loss may please be reimbursed to me in the form of compensation for incarceration without any wrongdoing.

Faithfully yours

APPENDIX C

Afghanistan, Damman near Kandahar Industrial Area
21 Oct. 2001
Author holding DU ammo bombshell scraps in Damman near Kandahar industrial area. Burden released by departing American jet after a bombing run on Kandahar

UTN team with visiting businessmen from Pakistan, stopped for refreshments
July, 2001
Suhail conducting a survey tour for interested Pakistani entrepreneurs and professionals on the road between Landikotal & Jalalabad. These tours were open for all nationalities

Surveying Dasht e Zarin land for development
May, 2001
UTN team and government officials outside Kandahar on Herat road where this 25 by 5 km land was allocated to UTN about 20 km from downtown Kandahar. The project was in its initial stages up until October 2001

UTN chief S B Mahmood in discussion with Ministry of Water and Power officials and UTN resident manager in Kabul Mr. Suhail
13 May, 2001
Inside Combined Cycle Power Plant left incomplete by Brown Bovary of Switzerland. It was taken up for completion by UTN. All parts required for completion were found on site

Destroyed Secondary Technical Education Institute
March 2001
Located just outside Khost. It was a flourishing institute before being
bombed to extinction in 1992 during the period of warlordism. It seemed
like a hobby with these warlords

Engineers and technicians at work
24 July 2001
Power and diesel workshop Kabul. Almost all machinery was patched
up for operations by Afghan engineers with UTN's help. Known as
Jugaar (make do) in a local dialect

Damaged Italian origin silo and flourmill
March 2001
this was located in Arghandab a suburb of Kandahar. Mill was
assessed to be beyond economical repairs due to extensive damage.
Used for target practice by all and sundry

Coming out of a mosque after noon prayers
May, 2001
From left: Big. Muhammad Ali, Chairman UTN S B Mahmood,
Consultant UTN Iqbal Mir and local Afghan officials. Pace of life was
unhurried easygoing

Foreign Office Guest House, Kandahar stay; group photo
May 2001
left to right: Big. Muhammad Ali, Mr. Yousuf Beg of Int'l Fabrication,
Engr. Rehan Faeeq, Mr. S M Tufail of FW Engineering, Mr. S B
Mahmood & local officials

Dasht e Zarin land allocated to UTN for development
August 2001
25 by 5 Km land strip along Kandahar- Herat road being worked.
Grapevines producing fruit are being surveyed. Afghan grapes were not
sour at that time for anyone. Not so sure now

Damaged Cotton Ginning & Extraction factory
June 2001
This factory was located about 150 km from Kandahar, off the Herat road. It was selected for rehabilitation by UTN. Most of such operations have been allowed to rust for now

Along the Kandahar- Heraat road
May,2001
Dasht e Zarin area just outside Kandahar, sparsely populated but with abundant ground water. It was surveyed by the Germans and then Russians for development

Khost Water Supply System
March, 2001
This water supply system was installed by the Germans in early 70's. It was partially destroyed and could be restored. UTN planned to upgrade it for operations up until 2025

Khost town, view from the water reservoir hill
March, 2001
Water reservoir tanks were located on the highest hill near town, from where this photo was taken. All gun emplacements had been removed from these hills

On a hill of iron ore
May, 2001
A member of survey team Eng. Yousaf Beg of UTN near Pul e Charkhi
iron ore deposits. He used a magnet to lift these stones

Approaches to copper, gold and iron ore deposits
May, 2001
UTN survey team member on a survey mission. Foot slogging was the
only way forward. No kind of transport could operate there

Pul e Khumri Cement Plant
July, 2001
Earmarked for expansion and modernization by UTN experts.
Uninstalled equipment was available on site. Production was low and
the staff uncooperative but competent

BBC Kabul Power Plant
May, 2001
UTN was completing this plant left unfinished by Brown Bovari of
Switzerland in Kabul. From left D G water and power, Mr. Iqbal Mir, and
Big. Muhammad Ali

Mazar e Sharif Fertilizer Plant
24 July, 2001
UTN was addressing the shortages due to technical personnel and maintenance spares. Small quantity of Urea and nitrates produced were going into agriculture

Khost to Kabul road
March, 2001
Remnants of rampart are visible. Road was completely gutted. There was no need to bomb the infrastructure. It was self destructing anyway

On the road from Kandahar to Kabul
March, 2001
Dirt track inside the river bed. Bridge was destroyed. Traffic continued on difficult alternate routes, even when there was water, during and after rare rains

Kandahar, destroyed infrastructure near city centre
September, 2001
The US & NATO forces attacked an already destroyed city on 07 October, 2001. Very expensive ammo was used to demolish such structures

Destroyed building somewhere in Kabul
September, 2001
An already destroyed city was attacked in October 2001 by Coalition
Forces causing immense suffering. These buildings were fit only to take
cover during street fighting

Kandahar Airport
October, 2001
Working and damaged Russian aircraft parked outside on a runway
before the attack on Kandahar on 07 October, 2001. These were
abandoned by them when they left in 1989

Kandahar Aerial bombing collateral damage. Darra Arghandhab
October, 2001
A civilian truck carrying groceries to market hit by a *precision guided* US missile killing the driver and cleaner. Such casualties were enormous because of lack of legitimate targets and shoddy ground intelligence

Plumes of smoke, Kandahar
October, 2001
Missiles hitting targets in Kandahar in early morning. Fires quickly extinguished because of lack of combustible materials. Fire fighting equipment was neither required nor used

Marble and onyx abundance near Lashkar Gah
August, 2001
These low hills comprising of marble and onyx were located north of Kandahar and near Lashkar Gah. Extraction was by wasteful blasting method. Most of it was being exported to Pakistan

Marble and Onyx Factory near Lashkar Gah
August, 2001
This factory was damaged and abandoned. All machinery installed was Italian and German origin. This operation could be restored and it was earmarked for rehabilitation

Flourmill in Kandahar Industrial Park
October, 2001
The almost complete flourmill as it stood just before the attack. Left untouched by attacking forces. The mill was visited thrice by US investigators after occupation. They took away flour samples for testing twice. It made good bread both times

One Body Flourmill in Kandahar City Centre
September, 2000
Set up in a damaged shed by a retired Pakistan Air Force officer with local collaboration. Got UTN thinking on these lines, resulting in a 200 tons/day capacity mill in about a year's time

GLOSSARY OF TERMS USED

ABC: American Broadcasting Corporation
AFIC: Armed Forces Institute of Cardiology: Premier cardiac care institute of Pakistan located in Rawalpindi.
AFP: Agence France Press
AI: Amnesty International
AP: Associated Press
AL QAEDA: First formed by Dr. Abdullah Azzam   in 1988. Later taken over by Osama Bin Laden in 1989; ostensibly to drive US forces out of Saudi Arabia.
BMR: Balancing, Modernization and Repairs
BBC: British Broadcasting Corporation
BBC: Brown Bovary Corporation: Brown Bovary Ltd of Baden, Switzerland. It merged with Asea AB of Vasteras, Sweden in 1987 to form a new Company, ABB (Asea Brown Bovary).
BOOT: Build Own Operate Transfer
CIA: Central Intelligence Agency
CNN: Cable News Network
COF: Coalition Occupation Forces: US, NATO and   ISAF forces which attacked and have partially   occupied Afghanistan since October, 2001.
Crore: = 1,000,000. Used in sub continental accounting system.
DCI: Director of Central Intelligence: Head of CIA
DG: Director General
DU: Depleted Uranium
ECL: Exit Control List: Maintained by the immigration department in the ministry of interior of   Pakistan, for persons not allowed to travel   internationally.
FAE: Fuel Air Explosive: A fuel dispenser bomb ignited in air after launch from aircraft. No more in widespread use.
FBI: Federal Bureau of Investigation

FIMA: Federation of Islamic Medical Associations: An umbrella organization based in Indiana, USA and constituted in December, 1981.

FO: Fibre Optic

GOA: Government of Afghanistan

GOP: Government of Pakistan

HRW: Human Rights Watch

I.B: Intelligence Bureau: An intelligence agency in the interior division of the GOP.

ICRC: International Committee of Red Cross

IED: Improvised Explosive Device: Any device set to explode remotely or in proximity when disturbed.

ISAF: International Security Assistance Force: Cobbled together by US to attack and occupy Afghanistan in October 2001.

ISI: Inter Services Intelligence: Premier intelligence service of Pakistan.

Jihad-e-Kashmir: Fortnightly published from Rawalpindi in Urdu.

KANUPP: Karachi Nuclear Power Plant: First nuclear power generation plant is a single unit CANDU PHWR generating 137 MW for Karachi city.

Lakh: = 100,000. Sub continental accounting system

LPG: Liquid Petroleum Gas

MIT: Massachusetts Institute of Technology: Located in Cambridge, Massachusetts, USA

MODC: Ministry of Defence Corp.: A constabulary force recruited by the Army for guard duties and security details in their establishments.

NA: Northern Alliance: Headed by Ahmad Shah Masood up until his death in 2001. Controlled 5% of Afghanistan in Badakhshan province opposing Taleban regime with Western support.

NATO: North Atlantic Treaty Organization

NGO: Non-Governmental Organization

NNI: News Network International

NWFP: North West Frontier Province: Now known as Pakhtunkhawa, to the north and west of Pakistan.

PAEC: Pakistan Atomic Energy Commission

PIMA: Pakistan Islamic Medical Association

PM:　　Prime Minister

PTCL: Pakistan Telecommunication Company Limited

RADAR: Radio Direction and Ranging: Use of radio waves to find range and direction in the air.

ROI:　　Return on Investment

S & T: Science and Technology

Sada-e- Shariah: Voice of Islamic tradition. Name given to Radio Afghanistan by Taleban

Seeh Murgh: A 4-wheel drive vehicle supplied to Mujahedeen by Pakistan during the Soviet invasion

SONAR:　Sound Navigation and Ranging: Use of sound waves to find range and direction in the sea.

STD: Sexually Transmitted Democracy: As in South   Asia, it runs in political families.

UN:　　United Nations

USSR: Union of Soviet Socialist Republics: Former name of the Russian Federation.

UTN:　Ummah Tameer-e- Nau: Set up in late 1999 to help alleviate poverty in Afghanistan and the   rest of the Muslim world.

WMD: Weapons of Mass Destruction

BIBLIOGRAPHY

1. *The Pathans* by Sir Olaf Caroe: first published in 1958 in the U.K. Tenth impression 1999.
2. *An Inquiry into the Culture of Power of the Subcontinent* by Ilhan Niaz: Alhamra Books, 2006. First impression
3. *A History of the Arab Peoples* by Albert Habib Hourani: 1991, the Belknap Press of Harvard University Press, Cambridge, Massachusetts, USA. First impression.
4. *A People's History of the United States* by Howard Zinn: published in1980, 1995, 1998, 1999, 2003. Harper Perennial Modern Classics, 2005.
5. *The Prince* by Niccolo Machiavelli: first published 1513. Bantam Classics edition 1981, translation by Daniel Donno with Discourses.
6. *In the Line of Fire* by Pervez Musharaff: first publication by Simon & Schuster in the U.K, 2006.
7. *Failure of Intelligence, The Decline and Fall of the CIA* by Melvin Allen Goodman: published in USA, 2008, by Rowman and Littlefield Publishers, Inc.
8. *At the Centre of the Storm, My years at the CIA* by George Tenet: Harper Collins Publishers, 2007, first edition.
9. *The Culture of Power and Governance of Pakistan, 1947- 2008* by Ilhan Niaz: Oxford University Press, 2010, first publication.
10. *Obama's War* by Bob Woodward: Simon & Schuster UK Ltd, 2010. First impression.
11. *The Looming Tower* by Lawrence Wright: Penguin Books, UK, 2007.
12. *Jihad-e- Kashmir,* fortnightly published from Rawalpindi and Muzaffarabad. 30 June,16 July,16 August, 31 August,16 September, 30 September, 16 October, 31 October, 16 November, 30 November, 16 December, 31 December, 2001 editions.
13. *Doomsday and Life after Death* by Sultan Bashir Mahmood. Darul Hikmat International, Islamabad, 1987.
14. *The Heirs of the Prophet Muhammad* (peace be upon him) by Barnaby Rogerson. First published in Britain in 2006 by Little, Brown. Reprinted 2007.
15. Documents and archival records, UTN from September, 1999 to December, 2001.

ABOUT THE AUTHOR

The author joined the Pakistan Navy in 1965. He was commissioned in the engineering branch of the Navy in 1969 and retired in 1993 after serving in various ships, submarines and shore establishments. He joined a large private company, in 1993, as managing director, manufacturing engine crankshafts with Spanish collaboration. In 2000 he joined an NGO, Ummah Tameer-e- Nau (UTN for short) to bring about an economic and technical union between Pakistan and Afghanistan by marrying the technical knowhow of the former with the natural resources of the later. The undertaking was in the national interest of both the countries. The book narrates briefly events which occurred from June 2000 to January 2002 as a result of that fateful decision.

ALSO AVAILABLE FROM
STRAND PUBLISHING

- *The Strand Book of Memorable Maxims*
- *The Strand Book of International Poets 2010*
- *The Strand Book of International Short Stories*
  (Suggestions for this series are welcome)

- *The Challenge of Reality* by Sultan Bashir Mahmood
- *The Path Of The Gods* by Joseph Geraci (entered The Criticos Prize, London 2010)
- *The First Casualty* by John Adam and MA Akbar
- *The Assassins Code 1* by Chrastopher Chance
- *The Misunderstood Ally* by Faraz Inam Siddiqui
- *The Box* by *Clive* Parker Sharp

~

All titles are available to order online from Amazon.co.uk and Amazon.com, Play.com, Tesco.com, WH Smiths, Waterstones, Blackwell, and all good booksellers and retailers.

To order copies direct from the publisher, or for more information about our books and services, visit our website:
www.strandpublishing.co.uk

Strand on Facebook:
http://www.facebook.com/pages/Strand-Publishing-UK-Ltd/294372581198?ref=sgm

Strand on Twitter:
http://twitter.com/#!/@strandpublishuk

CPSIA information can be obtained
at www.ICGtesting.com
Printed in the USA
2388LVUK00001B

9781907340130